The Reference Shelf®

Free Trade

Edited by Jennifer Peloso

Editorial Advisor Lynn M. Messina

The Reference Shelf
Volume 77 • Number 2

The H.W. Wilson Company
2005

The Reference Shelf

The books in this series contain reprints of articles, excerpts from books, addresses on current issues, and studies of social trends in the United States and other countries. There are six separately bound numbers in each volume, all of which are usually published in the same calendar year. Numbers one through five are each devoted to a single subject, providing background information and discussion from various points of view and concluding with a subject index and comprehensive bibliography that lists books, pamphlets, and abstracts of additional articles on the subject. The final number of each volume is a collection of recent speeches, and it contains a cumulative speaker index. Books in the series may be purchased individually or on subscription.

Library of Congress has cataloged this title as follows:

Free trade / edited by Jennifer Peloso; editorial advisor Lynn M. Messina
      p.cm.—(The reference shelf)
   Includes bibliographical references and index.
   ISBN 0-8242-1047-6
   1. Free trade. I. Peloso, Jennifer. II. Series

HF1713.F735 2005
382'.71—dc22

                        2005041573

On the cover: Workers at the Compasso Shoe Factory in Belo Horizonte, in the state of Minas Gerais, Brazil. (AP Photo/Washington Alves)

Visit H.W. Wilson's Web site: www.hwwilson.com

Printed in the United States of America

Contents

Preface

Since the North American Free Trade Agreement (NAFTA) was signed in 1994 by Canada, Mexico, and the United States, countries rich and poor have been scrambling to form their own free trade agreements (FTAs) in their regions of the world. Trade among nations has always been a cornerstone of economic policy, and the principles of free trade specifically have had both supporters and opponents. From corporate boardrooms to coal mines, college campuses to maquiladora factories, the headquarters of environmental activists to the seats of world governments, free trade agreements have been the subject of intense debate and close scrutiny. Why the enormous interest in and concern with FTAs at this time? That is one question we attempt to explore in this book.

The goal of FTAs is to eliminate tariffs and other trade barriers between mutually agreeing countries, opening up markets to foreign industries that had previously been shut out of those markets due to such impediments. From an economic standpoint, according to its advocates, free trade promises wealth and prosperity to all the nations involved, while politically, it fosters democracy and stability. Socially, its supporters argue, it brings a better way of life to people and increases standards of living, especially in developing or underdeveloped countries. It was these promises that persuaded the United States, Canada, and Mexico to sign NAFTA, the world's first international free trade agreement.

Since NAFTA went into effect on January 1, 1994, it has been considered the model for all succeeding FTAs. As the longest-running FTA to date, NAFTA provides the best evidence of an FTA's effects on the economies, politics, and societies of the countries involved. Opponents of FTAs, however, argue that NAFTA is a prime example of how FTAs do not achieve the goals their supporters promote. They cite the loss of American jobs to Mexico as one of the most distressing results of NAFTA, in addition to environmental degradation and the financial downfall of local industries in favor of corporate giants. If NAFTA is a blueprint for future FTAs, many feel the architects should go back to the drawing board. This book examines the debate surrounding free trade and FTAs with a special emphasis on NAFTA, as both supporters and detractors use specific examples from NAFTA's 10-year tenure to make their cases for and against future FTAs.

Chapter 1 provides a brief overview of topics that are discussed in greater depth throughout the rest of the book. A definition of free trade is provided, along with an examination of NAFTA and the effects it has had on the three signatory countries. The desire of the European Union and the developing world to enter into FTAs is analyzed, as is the idea of free trade versus fair trade.

As other countries consider entering into FTAs, they look to NAFTA as a prototype. Chapter 2 therefore takes a closer look at NAFTA's effects on industry, jobs, and the economies of the United States, Canada, and Mexico. Because Canada and the United States have similar free-market economies, and because so many trade agreements already existed between them prior to their entering into NAFTA, Canada is covered here less extensively than Mexico, which has been the most profoundly affected by NAFTA, both negatively and positively.

Although many in the United States have become disillusioned with NAFTA, primarily due to the relocation of some American businesses to Mexico (often to the detriment of local economies in the States) and what has been perceived as an imbalance of trade that has hurt Mexican farmers particularly, governments worldwide have continued to pursue FTAs. Chapters 3 and 4 examine other FTAs currently in the works, some of them fairly controversial. Chapter 3 focuses on FTAs in Latin America, while Chapter 4 takes a more global view and considers FTAs in areas such as Southeast Asia, the Middle East, and Australia.

Whereas the previous chapters discuss the economics and politics involved in free trade agreements, Chapter 5 delves into the social impact FTAs have on signatory nations. The effect of NAFTA on intellectual property laws, the environment, human rights, and women's rights is examined here and provides a glimpse into what the future may hold for other countries should new FTAs mirror NAFTA. The concluding chapter provides some scenarios for the future of NAFTA, as well as FTAs in regions like Latin America and other parts of the developing world.

My appreciation goes out to all the newspapers, journals, and other publications that granted us permission to reprint their articles in this volume. I would also like to thank Paul McCaffrey for his assistance in producing this book, as well as Michael Schulze, Norris Smith, Richard Stein, and Gray Young, who have supported and encouraged me in my work at Wilson. A special thanks goes out to Lynn Messina and Sandra Watson for their hard work, dedication, patience, and friendship in this endeavor and on other Wilson projects.

Jennifer Peloso
April 2005

I. Overview of Free Trade and NAFTA

Editor's Introduction

While economic theorists for centuries have debated the potential implications—both positive and negative—of trade without barriers, only recently have actual free trade agreements (FTAs) between countries been actively pursued and implemented. No longer just an academic abstraction, free trade is now a fact of life; indeed, it is the ascendant economic philosophy of the modern era. However, in recent years the limited implementation—and intellectual preeminence—of free trade has not quieted the debate between its proponents and detractors. Thus far the data yielded has not been compelling enough to quiet either side: Its adherents marshal evidence to claim that it is the best formula for economic growth and increased development, opening previously untapped markets to lucrative investment opportunities and improving the standard of living for all; meanwhile, free trade opponents contend that it cruelly exploits the weak and vulnerable and promotes the degradation of the environment simply to line the pockets of corporations and the wealthy. The North American Free Trade Agreement (NAFTA) remains at the center of the debate as those on both sides cite specific examples from its 10-year history to support their arguments regarding future FTAs.

Chapter 1 provides an overview of free trade, free trade accords, and the history of NAFTA, the first multilateral free trade agreement, including the views of its supporters and detractors. The chapter also looks at other regions of the globe, such as the European Union (EU) and the developing world, where FTAs have become increasingly common. The first article, "Free Trade," lays the thematic groundwork for the book, defining free trade while touching on some of the effects it has had on areas such as intellectual property. In addition, the piece briefly explains NAFTA's basic structure. The second article in this chapter, "Free Trade on Trial," takes a more in-depth look specifically at NAFTA, using the occasion of the accord's 10th anniversary to explore its impact thus far. In seeking to answer the question "Was NAFTA worth it?" the piece presents arguments from each side of the NAFTA debate while exploring the popularity of the agreement in the United States, Canada, and Mexico, as well as the economic impact it has had on all three countries.

Though Canada and Mexico are economically tied to the United States through NAFTA, they are also pursuing FTAs with other countries. The next article, "Connect the Markets," looks at the steps Canada and Mexico are taking to secure more FTAs around the world, especially with the EU. Many believe that countries need greater market access to raise themselves out of poverty. Free trade proponents theorize that FTAs offer the most effective means through which emerging nations can obtain such access. The next article in this chapter, "Annan, Silva Call for Using Free Trade to Raise Global Living Standards," looks at the rationale behind brokering FTAs between industrialized states and developing countries. It presents the potential implications that FTAs like these could have on the developing countries involved, not just economically, but in terms of infrastructure and technology as well.

As markets are opened through FTAs, many worry about the underlying fairness of these accords. The next article in this chapter examines "fair trade," a concept that has developed in response to certain inequities observed in the FTAs currently in use. Some have found that numerous countries, wealthy and impoverished alike, are so intent on entering into FTAs that they are willing to overlook sweatshop conditions and human rights abuses in their partner countries. In response, fair trade seeks to ensure that the benefits of free trade are shared by all and are not simply the provenance of the powerful and well-to-do. A sidebar accompanying the article outlines some of the issues that fair trade specifically addresses.

Free Trade

WIKIPEDIA, DECEMBER 11–16, 2004

Free trade is an economic concept referring to the selling of products between countries without tariffs or other trade barriers. Free trade is the absence of artificial (government-imposed) barriers to trade among individuals and firms in different nations. International trade is often constricted by different national taxes, other fees imposed on exported and imported goods, as well as non-tariff regulations on imported goods; theoretically, free trade is against all these restrictions. In reality, trade agreements that are labeled as "free trade" by their proponents may actually create their own barriers to a free market. Some critics of such trade agreements see them as protecting the interests of corporations.

Some multi-national entities, such as the European Union, have implemented free trade in some form between their member nations (customs union). However, there is continuing debate whether free trade would help third world nations with different economic problems and whether free trade is good for the developed world.

Arguments For and Against Free Trade

Many economists argue that free trade increases the standard of living through the theory of comparative advantage and economies of scale. Others argue that free trade allows developed nations to exploit developing nations, destroying local industry while circumventing social and labor standards. Conversely, some have argued that free trade hurts developed nations because it causes jobs from those nations to move to other countries with lower labor costs, producing a race to the bottom which causes a general lowering of health and safety standards.

Some descriptions of comparative advantage rest on a necessary condition of "capital immobility." If financial (or labor) resources can move between countries, then the comparative advantage theory erodes, and absolute advantage dominates. Given the liberalization of capital flows under free trade agreements of the 1990s, the condition of capital immobility no longer holds. As a consequence, it can be argued that the economic theory of comparative advantage no longer supports free trade theory. However, as economist Paul Krugman has noted, the 19th-century economic theorist David Ricardo, who formulated the well-known simple model of the comparative advantage doctrine, lived himself in a period of high capital mobility. Some take this to mean that the assumption of capital immobility in early models of the theory was merely an expositional convenience that is not essential to the principle. More complicated modern models of comparative advantage do include capital mobility (i.e., international borrowing, lending, and labor movement) and often posit movement of capital as analogous to the movement of goods.

> *Some suggest that free trade changes living conditions and careers too fast.*

In addition, the current implementation of free trade has been criticized by advocates of free trade itself. One complaint is that developed nations tend to insist that developing nations open their markets to industrial and agricultural products from the developed world, yet refuse to open their markets to agricultural goods from the developing world. A strong line of reasoning against free trade is that trade barriers such as quotas and agricultural subsidies prevent farmers in the third world from competing in local and export markets, thereby creating third-world poverty. Furthermore, it has been noted that the current concept of free trade supports the free movement of products and employers, which favors the developed nations, but not the free movement of employees (i.e., labor), which would favor the people of developing nations.

Some have argued that many of the alleged problems in the current free trade system, such as the race to the bottom and restriction of the movement of labor, would be eliminated by having a single world government with one law and no borders. This idea might be off-putting to some people on both sides of the argument and is thus rarely posited as a true solution.

Some suggest that free trade changes living conditions and careers too fast. Economic disruptions used to happen slowly enough that natural attrition, such as deaths and retirement, took care of the changes. One could finish his/her life as a farmer, yet his/her children could take up mining or manufacturing instead of farming. Now, changes happen on a sub-generation level, quicker than a natural-attrition rate, making coping very difficult, especially for those entering middle-age and the elderly.

Intellectual Property and Free Trade

Historically, the free trade movement was skeptical of and even hostile to the notion of intellectual property, which it regarded as monopolistic and harmful to a free, competitive economy. Indeed, during the late 19th century, free trade advocates succeeded in reducing the length of the patents available in many European countries. The Netherlands even abolished its patent system (temporarily, as it turned out).

The 19th-century anti-patent cause failed largely because the recession of 1874 discredited the free trade movement of the time (and also because patent advocates used a public relations campaign which was remarkably sophisticated for its time).

It is thus quite remarkable (some would even say ironic) that corporations lobbying for expanded intellectual property privileges have suc-

NAFTA has been contro-versial since it was first proposed.

ceeded in including TRIPS, a very strong treaty on intellectual property rights, as a membership requirement for the World Trade Organization, the international organization dedicated to furthering the cause of free trade.

North American Free Trade Agreement

The North American Free Trade Agreement, known usually as NAFTA, is a comprehensive trade agreement linking Canada, the United States, and Mexico in a free trade sphere. NAFTA went into effect on January 1, 1994.

The agreement immediately ended tariffs on some goods, and on other goods tariffs were scheduled to be eliminated over a period of time.

The agreement was an expansion of the earlier Canada–U.S. Free Trade Agreement of 1989. Unlike the European Union, NAFTA does not create a set of supranational governmental bodies, nor does it create a body of law which is superior to national law. NAFTA, as an international agreement, is very similar to a treaty (indeed, in Spanish, it is styled a *tratado*). Under United States law it is classed as a congressional-executive agreement.

The agreement was pursued by the Conservative governments in the U.S. and Canada. In Canada, the government was led by Brian Mulroney of the Progressive Conservative Party of Canada. The Canadian government worked aggressively with then-Republican president Ronald Reagan to create and sign the agreement. There was considerable opposition on both sides of the border that persists to today. Recently in Canada, labor unions have removed their objections to the agreement from their platforms.

Effects

NAFTA has been controversial since it was first proposed. Transnational corporations have tended to support NAFTA in the belief that lower tariffs would increase their profits. Labor unions in Canada and the United States have opposed NAFTA for fear that jobs would move out of the country due to lower wage costs in Mexico. Farmers in Mexico have opposed NAFTA because the heavy agriculture subsidies for farmers in the United States have put a great deal of downward pressure on Mexican agricultural prices, forcing many out of business. Opposition to NAFTA also comes from environmental, social justice, and other advocacy organizations that believe NAFTA has detrimental non-economic impacts to health, environment, etc. In Mexico, NAFTA's approval was quickly followed by an uprising among indigenous people led by the Zapatistas, and tension between them and the Mexican government remains a major issue.

Since NAFTA was signed, it has been difficult to analyze its macroeconomic effects due to the large number of other variables in the global economy. Various economic studies have generally indicated that rather than creating an actual increased trade, NAFTA has caused trade diversion, in which the NAFTA members now import more from each other at the expense of other countries worldwide.

From the perspective of North American consumers, the most prominent effect of NAFTA has been the significant increase in bilingual or even trilingual labeling on products, for simultaneous distribution through retailers in Canada, the U.S., and Mexico.

The Future

NAFTA Plus

Leaders from Canada, the United States, and Mexico are joining forces to establish a blueprint for a powerhouse North American trading bloc to compete with the rest of the world, shielded by a Fortress America–style defense perimeter.

A continent-wide customs-free zone with a common approach to trade, energy, immigration, law enforcement, and security that would virtually eliminate existing national borders has the total support of the three governments.

A continental energy accord is expected as well as special entry points for overseas travellers to North America while opening up most border crossings to relatively free passage of goods and citizens of the three countries—the first step into an EU-style pact in North America.

Free Trade on Trial

ECONOMIST, JANUARY 3, 2004

From the start, the North American Free Trade Agreement was bitterly controversial in all three of the countries taking part—the United States, Canada, and Mexico. Its terms, which went into effect on January 1, 1994, were argued over line by line: despite its name, the agreement fell far short of scrapping all trade restrictions, and the fine print of the various exemptions and exclusions gave rise to heated argument. More than this, the agreement was attacked as bad in principle. Everybody recognised that NAFTA was an extraordinarily bold attempt to accelerate economic integration—or, as critics put it, an experiment in reckless globalisation. As such, they said, it would destroy jobs, make the poor worse off, and start an environmental race to the bottom.

Equally, advocates of the agreement made some bold claims about the good it would bring. Far from destroying jobs, it would create lots of new and better ones; incomes would rise and the poor would benefit proportionately; growth would accelerate and, to the extent that this posed environmental challenges, extra resources would be available to meet them.

Unsurprisingly, a mere 10 years' experience has settled few of these quarrels. Today, most trade economists read the evidence as saying that NAFTA has worked: intra-area trade and foreign investment have expanded greatly. Trade sceptics and anti-globalists look at the same history and feel no less vindicated. Look at Mexico's growth since 1994, they say—dismal for much of the period. Look at the contraction of manufacturing employment in the United States. As for the environment, go to the places south of the border where the maquiladoras cluster, and take a deep breath.

Politically, the sceptics, 10 years on, can fairly claim victory. NAFTA is unpopular in all three countries. In Mexico, which stood to gain most from freer trade (since its barriers were so much higher at the outset) and which has indeed benefited greatly according to most economic appraisals, the agreement is widely regarded as having been useless or worse. In a poll conducted at the end of 2002 by Ipsos-Reid for the Woodrow Wilson Centre in Washington, only 29 percent of Mexicans interviewed said that NAFTA has benefited Mexico; 33 percent thought that it had hurt the country and 33 percent said that it had made no difference. In all three countries, the perceived results of NAFTA seem to have eroded support for further trade liberalisation.

NAFTA's champions are partly to blame for this: they oversold their case. It was never plausible, for instance, to expect that NAFTA would be a net creator of jobs. Trade policy is not a driver of overall employment; it affects the pattern of jobs, rather than the total number. To the extent that NAFTA succeeds in stimulating trade and cross-border flows of investment, jobs in each member country are created in some industries and destroyed in others. This was bound to be a painful process for some, even if it succeeded in making the member countries' economies more efficient overall, and hence in raising average incomes. Here was another instance of false advertising: NAFTA was never going to be, as some enthusiasts claimed, a win-win proposition for all of North America's citizens, even if all three countries could hope to gain in the aggregate.

> *It is pretty clear that NAFTA achieved as much as one could sensibly have expected it to achieve.*

Yes, It Worked

So far as its economic effects are concerned, the right question to ask of NAFTA is simply whether it indeed succeeded in stimulating trade and investment. The answer is clear: it did. In 1990 the United States' exports to, and imports from, Canada and Mexico accounted for about a quarter of its trade; now they account for about a third. That is a dramatic switch, especially when one notes that the United States' non-NAFTA trade has itself grown strongly over the period. There is plenty of economic evidence to suggest that expanded trade, as a rule, raises incomes and future rates of growth. So it is pretty clear that NAFTA achieved as much as one could sensibly have expected it to achieve.

Why then is the agreement so widely regarded by non-economists as a failure? The answer lies partly in the interplay of politics and economics, and accordingly is different in each of the member countries. But one theme is common to all three: a tendency to blame NAFTA in particular, and international integration in general, for every economic disappointment of the past 10 years, however tenuous the connection may be.

Debate in the United States has been preoccupied by fears over loss of jobs—by the "giant sucking sound" of work moving south, in Ross Perot's phrase from the early 1990s. A variety of estimates of NAFTA's direct effect on American labour have been made—with job losses running as high, according to one disputed study, as 110,000 a year between 1994 and 2000.

But, as already noted, direct losses do not tell the whole story: changing the pattern of employment is after all one of the reasons for promoting trade. So long as lost jobs are balanced by new ones, the overall effect on employment will be small. As Gary Hufbauer and Jeffrey Schott of the Institute for International Economics point out, between 1994 and 2000 the United States economy created more than 2 million new jobs a year. Manufacturing employment has dwindled (with NAFTA as one relatively minor cause among many); jobs in other industries have more than made up the losses. And since the mid-1990s, at any rate, the great majority of new jobs created have paid above-median wages.

Against this background, even NAFTA's highest estimated direct losses can hardly be regarded as crippling. America's evident disenchantment with liberal trade has less to do with the economic depredations of the 1990s—when the economy boomed, in fact—than with a political failure to make the case for free trade against its increasingly vocal and well-organised opponents.

In Canada, initial concerns were less to do with the flight of low-skilled manufacturing jobs, because trade with Mexico seemed a less pressing issue than it was for the United States, and more to do with other sorts of international competition. As it turned out, Canadian unemployment fell markedly during the 1990s (from 11 percent of the labour force in 1993 to 7 percent in 2000). The main fear, instead, was that closer integration with the American economy would threaten Canada's European-style social-welfare model, either by leading certain practices and policies (such as the generous minimum wage) to be regarded as directly uncompetitive, or else by pressing down on the country's base of corporate and personal taxes, thereby starving public-spending programmes of resources.

> *Even NAFTA's highest estimated direct losses can hardly be regarded as crippling.*

Canadian public spending was indeed squeezed somewhat during the 1990s—not because NAFTA eroded the tax base, but because public borrowing had reached an unsustainable level of 8 percent of GDP in the early 1990s. The problem was successfully addressed: Canada has lately run a budget surplus. Despite the fiscal retrenchment, and despite NAFTA, its social-welfare model stands intact, and in sharp contrast with that of the United States. The fact is, most Canadians are willing to pay the higher taxes that are required to finance generous public services (including universal health care). As long as this remains true, NAFTA poses no threat to the Canadian way of life.

Down South

What about Mexico? The very point of NAFTA, to listen to some of its advocates, was to destroy the Mexican way of life and replace it with something better. The overall verdict on NAFTA rests heavily on whether the pact proved a success for the country it was bound to affect most. NAFTA was never going to have much impact on the huge economy of the United States. But as recently as the mid-1980s Mexico was still an almost completely closed economy. For Mexico, NAFTA promised to be revolutionary.

Unfortunately, soon after NAFTA came into effect, the country was overwhelmed by a largely unrelated economic shock, the Tequila crisis of 1994–95. Huge capital inflows into the country in the early 1990s were followed by rapid outflows towards the end of 1994, causing the peso to plunge. The authorities were forced to float the currency on December 20th of that year, and before long it had lost nearly half of its value against the dollar.

The financial system collapsed, with many banks going under as years of bad loans were exposed. In the end, at huge cost, the government had to bail out the banks. The repercussions of the Tequila crisis for Mexico were immense. The banks, for instance, have still not fully recovered, and the subsequent lack of credit and financial services does much to explain the anaemic performance of Mexico's domestic economy over the past decade. All this makes judging the effects of NAFTA very difficult.

Take real wages. Although Mexican workers have managed impressive gains in productivity over the past 10 years to compete with America and Canada, real wages have not kept pace. This allows NAFTA's critics to argue that the typical Mexican has not benefited from the treaty as he should have done, and that big business has creamed off most of the profits.

The truth is different. The Tequila crisis led to an immediate fall of about 20 percent in Mexican wages (more in dollar terms), while productivity kept going up. So although real wages have been rising ever since the country began to recover in 1996, they are only just reaching their levels of before the crisis. The lasting influence of higher productivity on wages may not be clear for another decade, when the effects of the Tequila crisis have fully faded away. That said, the country recovered much more quickly from the Tequila crisis than from its previous financial crises in 1982 and 1986—and this was indeed mainly due to NAFTA. Speedily arranged help from Bill Clinton's administration spurred the strong recovery. That aid sprang from America's desire not to let its new partner go under.

The closeness of the link to America, the destination of almost 90 percent of Mexican exports, is of course a disadvantage when America goes into recession, as it did in 2001. Mexico lost thousands of export jobs in that downswing. On the other hand, NAFTA has insulated Mexico against the financial instability that swept through Argentina, Brazil, and other parts of South America in the first years of the new century. It has given Mexico an investment grade credit rating, and allowed it to issue—almost uniquely in Latin America—very long-term local-currency bonds and mortgage-backed securities. Investors now think of Mexico more as a North American than a Latin American country.

Former President Carlos Salinas de Gortari embraced NAFTA mostly to attract more foreign investment and to boost the maquiladora manufacturers (set up in 1965 to allow tariff-free import of materials for assembly and re-export to the United States). Mexico's trade has surged, especially with the United States. In 2002 it totalled $250 billion, and the country's traditional deficit with its northern neighbour has been converted into a surplus in every year of NAFTA membership.

After 1994 foreign direct investment also shot up. NAFTA was designed to make investors feel more legally secure, and foreign companies duly poured in to take advantage of Mexico's

Mexico has no shortage of problems that NAFTA has so far failed to solve.

closeness to the world's wealthiest market. The rise in export manufacturing also greatly reduced the country's dependence on the volatile price of oil. Moreover, NAFTA jobs in export businesses have usually been good ones, paying on average substantially more than jobs in the rest of the economy.

It hardly needs saying, however, that Mexico has no shortage of problems that NAFTA has so far failed to solve. One is the challenge of providing decently paid work for all those who need it. The chief symptom of the failure to do that, of course, is the continuing outflow of migrants.

The biggest pressure on emigration, in turn, is the crisis in the countryside. The traditional Mexican farmer had about eight hectares of his own land and some communal land for livestock. This made his family self-sufficient in everything from maize and beans to meat and milk. Even before NAFTA this traditional rural economy was disappearing, as demographic pressure caused the land to be subdivided, and many campesinos now eke out a living year by year, ever on the edge of disaster. "If the weather does not help us, we are completely lost," says Dionisio Garcia, who farms a small holding in the southern state of Tlaxcala.

Most of Mr. Garcia's colleagues have simply given up. He estimates that up to 90 percent of the heads of families in his area now spend at least six months of the year working in Canada or the United States. "What they earn there in four months, we don't earn here in a year," he says. They are part of an estimated 1.3 million people who have left the land since 1994. The young, besides, are no longer much interested in making a living from the land; they are going off to drive taxis in the city, or to sell air-conditioners.

Mr. Garcia says that he can no longer sell his surplus maize to Mexican wholesalers because he has been undercut by cheaper and better American imports. For him, NAFTA and free trade have been "totally bad." And yet trade in Mexico's two staples, maize and beans, is still not free; the last tariffs will remain until 2008.

The flood of corn from America's midwest is the most hated aspect of NAFTA for Mexicans. The government argues that it has to import so much because Mexico's small farmers cannot feed all Mexicans, let alone turn a profit. But critics allege that Americans are selling so cheap that they are, in effect, dumping the stuff. Besides, they receive vast subsidies from their government. NAFTA explicitly pledges to eliminate these, but it has not done so yet.

Some Mexican farmers have shown that they can make a good living under NAFTA. Export earnings from horticulture have tripled since 1994, to over $3.5 billion; exports of fresh vegetables have risen by 80 percent and fresh fruit by 90 percent. If farmers can exploit local conditions and invest in a crop that can be exported during American or European winters, they can make money. The star performer is the Hass avocado from the state of Michoacán, in the west of Mexico, where the climate is mild and the soil fertile. Before NAFTA, the United States banned it because of infestation by insects. After a clean-up and monitoring operation, supervised under NAFTA rules, avocados from Michoacán were accepted into most states of America in 1997. Exports have increased from 6,000 tonnes to 30,000 tonnes a year.

Overall, though, Mexico continues to rely on low-cost assembly, and the advantage of preferential entry into the American market. Increasingly, other countries offer cheaper labour; with China's accession to the World Trade Organisation, Mexico has already lost much of the advantage that NAFTA gave it. Many Mexicans still think that a reviving American economy, by itself, can buoy their own. But in the next upswing, as America deepens its trade links with other states, this may prove untrue.

NAFTA alone has not been enough to modernise the country or guarantee prosperity. It was never reasonable to suppose that it would be—though that did not stop many of its advocates saying so. NAFTA has spurred trade for all its members. That is a good thing. But trade can do only so much. Sadly, successive Mexican governments have failed to deal with the problems—corruption, poor education, red tape, crumbling infrastructure, lack of credit, and a puny tax base—that have prevented Mexicans and foreign investors alike from exploiting the openings which freer trade afforded. Don't blame NAFTA for that.

Connect the Markets

By Alan M. Field
Journal of Commerce, August 30, 2004

The United States isn't the only nation that's signing bilateral trade agreements. These deals are proliferating, often fueled by politics, national pride, and a desire by nations to show that they aren't dependent on the U.S. It's a worldwide trend, and examples are as close as Canada and Mexico. Headlines this summer in Canada have highlighted a dispute with a Spanish-led consortium that wants to raise tolls on the Ontario highway it operates. The leader of the consortium, Ferrovial SA, was reportedly pressuring Madrid to veto European Union approval of a trade and investment agreement with Canada, if Ferrovial didn't get its way. The stakes were high because the agreement was viewed as a major effort by Canada to reduce its dependence on the U.S.—something that has long been an issue in Canada.

At a summit meeting last May in Guadalajara, Mexico, leaders of 58 European Union, Latin American, and Caribbean countries called for a "multilateral" strategy to counteract U.S. influence by strengthening trade and investment ties between European countries and Latin America. Spanish prime minister Jose Luis Zapatero called for a "common front" against the U.S. French president Jacques Chirac told the summit, "Multilateralism is an imperative of our times." The urge to bypass U.S. influence was supported by sentiment against U.S. policy in Iraq.

Multilateralism is not new, especially for the EU, which has signed a wide range of trade agreements throughout the world, including a free trade pact with Mexico in 2000. Equally significant, Mexico recently negotiated a free trade pact with Japan that is scheduled to take effect Jan. 1. Multilateralism is not new, especially for the EU, which has signed a wide range of trade agreements throughout the world, including a free trade pact with Mexico in 2000.

Though many of these deals are rooted more in politics than in commerce, they will have commercial impact. With most tariffs now controlled by World Trade Organization negotiations, many bilateral trade agreements are focused on lowering trade-facilitation and investment barriers between nations or trading blocs. The effects won't be dramatic, but the deals could open opportunities for companies' sourcing.

An example: The soon-to-be-implemented agreement between Mexico and Japan. Under the deal, Japan eventually will eliminate tariffs on 95 percent of its imports from Mexico, and will open its market to several Mexican agricultural commodities. In return, Mexico will liberalize tariffs on Japanese automobiles after seven years, abolish steel tariffs in 10 years, and allow Japanese businesses to bid on Mexican government contracts of more than $10 billion.

The Mexico-Japan FTA could stimulate investment by Japanese manufacturers who see Mexico as a low-cost alternative to China. Alberto de la Pena, an international trade lawyer at Haynes and Boone in Dallas, said it will help the U.S. "because Mexico gives the Japanese manufacturers one more option to produce outside the United States—but closer to the U.S." It also might make it easier for a U.S. company to manufacture a product in Mexico and export it to Japan. By lowering trade and investment barriers, bilateral

---

Flexibility has become more important as companies adopt global sourcing strategies, supplying markets from countries where goods can be produced most efficiently.

---

accords such as the one between Mexico and Japan will provide U.S. companies with more flexibility in managing their global supply chains.

This flexibility has become more important as companies adopt global sourcing strategies, supplying markets from countries where goods can be produced most efficiently. Several companies, including Xporta, NextLinx, Vastera, and Open Harbor, use computers to crunch import tariffs and other costs and advise companies on the optimum places to source products. As trade barriers fall, this business is expanding rapidly.

Some of the new bilateral agreements fall into the category of "new-age" trade pacts. Despite the headlines about free trade, the EU-Canada negotiations scheduled for this fall will not aim to create a full-fledged trade agreement. Although the talks will cover issues of trade facilitation (including customs practices) and government procurement, they will focus on removing regulatory barriers that thwart trade and investment.

"Tariffs are no longer a problem between Canada and Europe; most tariffs are gone. But the Europeans are masters at building non-tariff barriers into the system," said Tom d'Aquino, president and chief executive of the Canadian Council of Chief Executives, which represents Canadian companies.

D'Aquino said stronger ties between Canada and Europe will remove barriers—and smooth supply chains—for U.S. companies doing business in Canada and Europe, not undermine them. "This idea that if you do a trade agreement on your left side, you are taking away something from your right side—that is baloney," he said.

D'Aquino said the Canada-EU talks will not aim to reduce Canada's dependence on the U.S. "It is wrongheaded to argue that Canada should seek alternative trade and investment relationships in order to reduce its dependence on the U.S. We have a 19 percent share of the U.S. import market, and I see this fact as a huge opportunity and economic catalyst. Our relationship with the U.S. is a huge asset for us, and we should make no apologies for it."

Surveys show Canadian companies are interested in removing European regulatory bottlenecks to Canadian exports in such manufacturing sectors as chemicals, agriculture, and food. Although Canada is enjoying enormous success in Europe's service sector, it has been less successful exporting manufactured goods to Europe. Last year, the EU bought 17 percent of Canada's total exports of

---

"The lion's share of Mexico's trade is now governed by the preferential rules of FTAs."—**Naoko Munakata, Center for Northeast Asian Policy Studies**

---

services, but the EU purchased only 5.6 percent of Canada's total exports of goods.

In recent years, Mexico has negotiated 32 free trade agreements, including deals with the EU in 2000 and with Japan. But these deals have hardly proved a panacea. The Inter-American Development Bank reported in May that Mexican exports to Europe have fallen significantly since the EU agreement, after rising sharply during the 1990s before the free trade pact with Europe took effect. Mexico's trade deficit with the EU increased from $7.5 billion in 1999 to $12.3 billion in 2003. That figure was the equivalent of nearly double Mexico's global trade deficit of $6.2 billion last year.

From the European perspective, the free trade pact with Mexico has also failed to work wonders. However, it has helped reverse the declining share of the Mexican market that Europe experienced after the North American Free Trade Agreement, the IADB report said. In 2000, the EU accounted for 8.5 percent of Mexico's total imports. By 2003, that share had grown to 10.5 percent.

By 2007, all Mexico-EU trade in industrial goods—some 93 percent of bilateral trade—will be tariff-free. Although barriers on bilateral investment flows began only last year, the IADB report is pessimistic about the impact of the EU-Mexico agreement on European investment in Mexico.

The new Mexico-Japan free trade pact is also likely to have limited impact. At best, it will stimulate lagging Japanese investment in Mexico's industrial sector—especially in the automobile sector.

Japanese manufacturers have been losing market share in Mexico because of Mexico's 32 free trade pacts, which improve access for those partners. A report by Japan's Ministry of Economy, Trade, and Industry blames tariff rates that average 16 percent on Mexican imports from Japan.

Mexico's roster of free trade partners includes not only Japan and the U.S. and Canada—within the North American Free Trade Agreement—but the EU, Israel, and countries throughout Central and South America. "The lion's share of Mexico's trade is now governed by the preferential rules of FTAs," said Naoko Munakata, a visiting fellow at the Center for Northeast Asian Policy Studies.

Japan's agreement with Mexico is only Japan's second bilateral free trade agreement, following one signed with Singapore in 2002. However, the Japan-Mexico FTA will be the first Japanese free trade pact that covers all areas of trade, including agriculture.

The new trade pact will allow Mexico to "somewhat unlink our exports for the economic cycle of just one market: the United States," according to Mexico's Economy Ministry. The ministry projects that Mexico's exports to Japan will grow at an annual rate of 10.6 percent, and directly generate 277,000 new Mexican jobs over the next decade. If so, that will be good news for all companies serving the Mexican market. The ministry projects that Japan's foreign direct investment in Mexico will average $1.3 billion a year over the next decade.

The Japan-Mexico pact could also boost Japan's efforts to negotiate free trade pacts with Asian countries—and sell the long-controversial concept of free trade at home. Munakata said Japan can easily see in Mexico the disadvantages of remaining an outsider in the era of free trade pacts.

U.S. officials are equally confident that if the EU-Canada talks remove regulatory barriers to bilateral trade and investment, the results will benefit U.S. companies in Europe, where the U.S. is in parallel discussions about removing regulatory barriers. "We don't oppose any agreement that lowers barriers or opens markets," said Richard Mills, a spokesman for the U.S. Trade Representative. "We cannot go out and do our aggressive free trade agreements and then criticize others for doing this sort of thing."

Canada's Tom d'Aquino said the overall effect is positive: "Every time an agreement results in the lowering of barriers, it is diluting protectionism worldwide."

Annan, Silva Call for Using Free Trade to Raise Global Living Standards

By Alan Clendenning
Associated Press, June 15, 2004

Amid calls from poor countries for the elimination of agricultural subsidies, U.N. secretary-general Kofi Annan urged representatives of 180 nations to push for free trade agreements that will raise global living standards.

"Let us help developing countries take full advantage of trading opportunities," Annan said Monday at the opening of the United Nations Conference on Trade and Development. "And let us find our way to a development-led approach to trade and other policies that will enrich and empower all the world's peoples."

Brazilian president Luiz Inaci Lula da Silva, who became a strong voice on free trade issues after taking office last year, said the developing world should learn how to use globalization instead of denouncing it.

While activists condemn globalization as unfettered free trade that benefits multinational corporations, Silva said it can be harnessed—to help poor countries gain greater market access, eliminate misery, and obtain funding to improve infrastructure and technology.

"Globalization is not synonymous with development, it is not a substitute for development, but it can be used as an instrument for development," said Silva, Brazil's first elected leftist leader.

The forum is bringing together ministers of the world's richest and poorest countries in São Paulo, Brazil's financial and industrial capital, amid the tightest security the city has ever seen. Thousands of soldiers toting semiautomatic rifles are posted at street corners and on overpasses.

Thai prime minister Thaksin Shinawatra said poor countries must drop their own barriers to mutual trade instead of waiting for international agreements that could give them better access to the markets of their richer counterparts.

"Given the increasingly zero-sum attitude of the north towards trade, we should diversify our risk by exploring more opportunities in the south," Thaksin said.

Silva, echoing the views of many conference delegates, said poor countries will grab a larger share of world trade if they can find ways to reduce barriers among themselves.

He said 44 developing countries who signed the Global System of Trade Preferences will hold new talks on reducing tariffs. Silva also said he hopes to enlist 40 new member countries from the developing world.

They could also use advances as a way to put pressure on richer countries to get rid of trade barriers.

The GSTP accord "lets developing countries eliminate reciprocal commercial barriers without the need of extending the same concessions to the developed world," Silva said.

Humanitarian groups welcomed Silva's announcement, but warned that sudden liberalization of free trade between developing countries could hurt the world's poorest nations.

While Brazilian farmers use advanced technology, millions of Indian farmers could be wiped out if Brazilian agricultural products flooded India, said Katia Maia of Oxfam International.

"Less developed countries must retain the right to protect vulnerable farm sectors and infant industries."—Katia Maia, Oxfam International

---

"Less developed countries must retain the right to protect vulnerable farm sectors and infant industries," she said.

But forum delegates said the elimination of agricultural trade advantages in wealthy countries would translate into a better life for destitute farmers with few other employment possibilities.

Their most bitter complaint: Generous subsidies in the United States and the European Union that give farmers a big competitive advantage over producers from poor countries.

Several hundred anti-globalization protesters marched Monday to a police barricade near the forum site in a sprawling convention center surrounded by legions of riot police and newly erected metal fences to protect the delegates.

"We're not terrorists!" organizers yelled from a sound truck rigged with huge speakers as they approached the barricade. "The terrorists are hunger, misery, free trade, and WTO deals!"

UNCTAD held its last forum in Bangkok, Thailand, in 2000 just months after the WTO's attempt to launch a new round of trade negotiations in Seattle collapsed amid violent anti-globalization street protests.

Top trade officials met on the sidelines of the São Paulo conference over the weekend in a push to break down global trade barriers under the auspices of the 147-nation WTO.

They said they made progress toward ending an impasse on agricultural subsidies in developed countries, but still must resolve many technical details before a July deadline in the stalled Doha round aimed at slashing the subsidies, tariffs, and other barriers.

Negotiators for the EU and the Mercosur bloc of South American countries—Argentina, Brazil, Paraguay, and Uruguay—continued talks Monday on their bid to create a free trade zone.

The two sides are still far apart on the key issues of agricultural subsidies, services, and government procurement ahead of an October deadline for a deal.

What Can We Do?

Geographical Magazine, February 2004

To Western consumers, international trade is largely invisible. But the chances are that every time you make a cup of coffee, put on a pair of shoes, or plug in your laptop computer, you are using things made by people in developing countries. Yet the money they receive for producing these goods represents only a tiny proportion of the final retail price; this situation has led to allegations of sweat-shop profiteering against major sports-shoe and clothing brands. The rapper P. Diddy was recently criticised when a Honduran worker from a factory that supplies his designer Sean John brand complained of brutality and slave-like conditions. It was also revealed that workers were paid as little as 15 cents to sew men's shirts that then retailed for $40 in New York.

Another major issue is the decreasing prices of primary produce. Coffee, for example, has fallen to a 30-year low on international markets because of over production, with prices halving in the past three years. Having already invested time and money in planting and cultivating coffee trees—which can take as long as four years to start bearing fruit—farmers in poor countries have little choice but to go ahead and sell anyway—at a big loss. This crisis hasn't hit the multinational coffee-roasting companies, however, which are raking in enormous profits on the back of low prices and the popularity of high-street cafe chains such as Coffee Republic and Starbucks. The result is that coffee farmers today receive less than one per cent of the price of the average cappuccino.

These inequalities have helped spark the burgeoning fair-trade movement, for which coffee has long been a pioneering product. Brands such as Cafédirect are now available in major supermarkets, as well as more niche outlets such as Oxfam shops. In 2002, after years of being lobbied, even Starbucks came on board: it declared its intention to obtain all of its coffee from sources that met new social and environmental guidelines and offered to purchase most of its beans at fixed, long-term prices. Fair trade can have a major impact in improving people's lives. As Felipe Huaman, a grower with the Bagua Grande Cooperative in Peru, explains: "Ever since we formed our alliance with Twin and Cafédirect, our prices have started improving, and this has improved living conditions for the coffee growers' families. This is our biggest reward and what we most appreciate."

Consumers are increasingly opting for more ethical coffee: fair-trade sales worldwide grew by 12 per cent in 2001, while overall coffee consumption increased by just 1.5 per cent. In the UK, fair-trade roast and ground coffee has now captured seven per cent of the market, and the Cafédirect brand now ranks sixth in terms of sales. This massive growth has also been paralleled elsewhere in

No matter how bright the future, fair trade remains a tiny niche market.

the fair-trade movement. Globally, around 4.5 million producers and their families are now thought to be benefiting from fair trade in 36 of the world's poorest countries. Fair-trade food sales are now growing internationally at more than 25 per cent a year; they increased in Britain by 90 per cent over the past two years. One-and-a-half million fair-trade bananas are now sold every week in the UK, and shoppers spent £63 million at the checkout on foods with the Fairtrade Mark in 2002. Fair-trade food products now include mangoes, oranges, pineapples, cocoa, sugar, honey, biscuits, snack bars, chocolate, tea, jams, and chutney.

Fair trade is moving into schools, companies, and local authorities and is backed by rock bands such as Radiohead and Coldplay. London's mayor, Ken Livingstone, recently pledged his support to efforts to make the capital a "fair-trade city." "I believe that a world city has world responsibilities," he said. "The food and drink we consume is more than just a commodity or luxury—it affects the lives of millions of people in developing countries." On a broader scale, leading UK charities, trade unions, and retailers have set up the Ethical Trading Initiative, which has established a code of conduct for its members, which include Marks and Spencer, Debenhams, and Sainsbury's.

"Fair trade is inexorably moving mainstream," says Harriet Lamb, director of the Fairtrade Foundation. "Our aim is to make the products available everywhere—supermarkets, work canteens, coffee bars, corner shops, hotels, bed and breakfasts, healthfood shops, hospitals, wherever. More and more people want to choose it, but they can't unless they are offered it."

But no matter how bright the future, fair trade remains a tiny niche market, and its total annual value of £63 million is no more than the turnover of a single large supermarket. Moreover, although fair trade has shown that you don't need charity to lift people out of poverty, it does little to challenge wider inequalities of the world trading system. So although Western consumers may have developed a taste for guilt-free food, the wider campaign against unfair trade goes on.

Fair Trade Hot Buttons

By Celeste Fraser Delgado, Tristram Korten, and Rebecca Wakefield
Miami New Times, November 13, 2003

Market Access

This issue puts the "free" in free trade by tearing down the barriers between nations and letting goods flow unfettered across borders. The current draft mandates that member countries eliminate tariffs on all imports from other member countries within 10 years after the FTAA [Free Trade Area of the Americas] goes into effect. Taxing exports or limiting exports in any other way is a no-no, even if a government is trying to fight a food shortage or wants to keep at home vital natural resources such as gas or water. To give everyone in the Americas equal access to all markets, all "nontariff trade barriers" must go too. So, for example, there can be no national environmental or health restrictions on goods entering the country, says the draft, that are "more restrictive of trade than necessary."

Government Procurement

From staplers to tanks, if a government needs something, it must give every company across the Americas a fair shot at making the sale. And we're not just talking about national governments, but provincial, state, and municipal governments as well. So no more sweetheart deals for a close relative's firm. No special consideration for goods made in the 'hood. Unless a government wants to risk being sued for presenting an "unnecessary barrier to trade," the only criteria to be used when evaluating a contract will be price and quality. That means no national government can exclude goods from another nation as a way of protesting, say, human-rights abuses. Good thing for el exilio Cuba is cut out from the get-go, or there'd be no more embargo.

Intellectual Property Rights

From now on, when we say "patent" or "copyright" anywhere in the Americas, we mean it. As the draft now stands, music pirates—whether street-corner cassette peddlers or sophisticated file-sharers—can do jail time. But intellectual property doesn't end with artistic creations. The FTAA extends patent protection to organic material like genetically altered seeds and to lifesaving drugs as well. So farmers can be busted if they don't kick the habit of saving seeds from previous harvests to plant the next crop. And companies making generic drugs, like the cheap AIDS treatments made and sold in Brazil, may have to go through costly drug trials as a way of making competition with the big pharmaceutical companies fair. Given how much some member nations depend on generic drugs to care for citizens who are sick and poor, there's a proposal for allowing states to grant licenses to generic companies without trials, but the United States at present is opposed to such a provision.

Services

May I help you? Then whatever I do for you is fair game for free trade. The free flow of trade applies not only to tangible goods—stereos, surfboards, submarines—but to services as well. That means the stuff we're used to getting from private companies, like banking, insurance, telecommunications, and tourism. And other things some of us are accustomed to getting from the government: water, education, police protection, library services, healthcare, unemployment checks. If a government wants to be piggy about public service and deliver the goods all by itself, it will run afoul of the rules for free trade and will likely pay a hefty price to any company who feels left out. Some of the smaller countries don't like this rule at all, so there is debate over whether small economies could be exempt from opening their national markets for services.

Agriculture

This is a major sticking point between the United States and the nations to the south. The goal is to eliminate all "export subsidies," but export subsidies come in many guises. In the United States, powerful interests in steel, citrus, and sugar don't want to give up the domestic dole they've enjoyed for decades. Still that's not the only source of disagreement. Other countries are picky about allowing genetically modified foods within their borders—but regulations against such foods could be considered an "export subsidy" for domestic goods. The same goes for such "export subsidies" as any domestic laws that allow a country to control the food supply or price by stockpiling foodstuff.

Investment

The aim is to create a stable and predictable business environment throughout the hemisphere to protect the investor and the investment. This is necessary, goes the argument, in less stable countries where assets could be unilaterally seized. To provide recourse, foreign corporations would be given "most-favored nation" status and protected under "national treatment" clauses. The concern is that foreign companies would be able to challenge a nation's regulations such as social and environmental standards. And this is where the NAFTA Chapter 11 model would apply: Foreign companies would be allowed to sue governments over regulations that affect their profits. Opponents claim that settling disputes in this way circumvents a country's legal system and is skewed toward big business.

Antidumping and Countervailing Measures

The FTAA wants to prevent the sale of products in another country at less than fair market value. The problem is figuring out what fair market value is. What one country complains is "too cheap," another counters is simply a reflection of higher productivity or lower labor costs. Whoever you believe, the language here is now so squishy as to be meaningless. If the negotiators can come up with clear language, this provision could level the playing field between big countries and the little guys.

Dispute Settlement

If the FTAA goes into effect, how will the new rules be enforced? If government A accuses government B of breaking the rules, then A can challenge any of B's laws, programs, or policies that appear to violate the FTAA. An FTAA panel would decide if there is in fact a violation. If there is, government B has three choices: change its laws; pay compensation to A; or risk heavy trade sanctions from the rest of the member countries. But a company doesn't need to get its own government on board to sue another country for violating the FTAA. Resorting to the investment rules, a company can sue another country directly for lost profits. A corporation can, for example, make a government pay to compensate for any profits lost due to domestic environmental or health regulations.

Competition Policies

Free trade means all trade, so if a government tries to keep a monopoly over a certain national market—whether that's oil or education—foreign firms and investors have a right to sue for a piece of the action through a supra-national body the FTAA would set up. That doesn't mean an end to all state-run businesses; it just means that any business run by the state must allow for open competition. Critics worry that such privatization would hit the poor and the civil service, who depend on state enterprise, the hardest.

II. NAFTA's Effects on Industry and Jobs

Editor's Introduction

The implementation of NAFTA by the United States, Canada, and Mexico raised a number of concerns among its opponents. As trade barriers were erased, some worried that U.S. companies were going to take advantage of cheap Mexican labor and lax environmental laws and move their factories across the border. Former presidential hopeful Ross Perot even warned of a "giant sucking sound" as American jobs were relocated to Mexico. At the same time, NAFTA skeptics argued that trade barriers protected American industries; without them, they predicted, U.S. markets would be flooded by a huge wave of cheap Mexican imports. Conversely, critics wondered how the small Mexican farmer would survive when forced to compete with his heavily subsidized American counterpart. More generally, skeptics questioned whether NAFTA would provide any real benefit to those on the lower rungs of the socioeconomic ladder or if it would simply prove a boon to the wealthy.

Ten years after NAFTA was implemented, a great deal of analysis has emerged concerning these issues, particularly in regards to the accord's impact on specific industries and on employment in general. This chapter focuses on how NAFTA has changed individual industries as well as how organized labor has fared under the agreement. In addition, the chapter analyzes how exactly the transformations brought about by NAFTA have restructured the economies of the three countries.

The opening piece, "Integrating the North American Steel Market," examines the ramifications for the U.S. steel industry of Mexican and Canadian steel "dumping" and how that issue was resolved. It also highlights the differences in the way free trade is implemented in the steel industry under NAFTA as opposed to its execution under the accords of the European Union. Although antidumping laws were written to prevent a repeat of the steel industry's problem in other sectors, similar impasses have developed. The second article in this chapter, "Time to Bury the Hatchet," discusses a recent conflict involving the U.S. and Canadian lumber industries.

While some U.S. industries are adversely affected by NAFTA rules, others flourish under them. The American auto and agricultural industries in particular have experienced NAFTA's integration of the three markets as a considerable advantage. The benefits reaped by these industries are documented in the next two articles, "NAFTA Contributing to Car Industry Success" and "NAFTA's Impacts on U.S. Agriculture: Trade & Beyond."

Although U.S. agriculture has thrived under NAFTA, Mexican growers—especially hog farmers—have not been so lucky. "NAFTA Sprouts Mexico Woe," the fifth entry in this chapter, discusses the specific concerns Mexican farmers have about the removal of tariffs and the ensuing flood of U.S. agricultural products. Mexican farmers cite U.S. federal subsidies as a major impediment to fair competition and have called on their government to level the playing field by providing similar support to them. The "squeeze" being put on many Mexican farmers is forcing them to look for jobs illegally across the border, they claim.

The "Symposium" that follows asks the question, "Has NAFTA been a good deal for the average worker?" In the first half of the piece, Daniel T. Griswold answers in the affirmative, citing specific examples of how U.S. and Mexican workers have benefited from the agreement. William R. Hawkins offers a vivid counterpoint in the second half of the article, arguing that NAFTA has slowed the economy and thus caused the loss of U.S. jobs. A sidebar discussing some of the major provisions of NAFTA is included.

In "Economists See NAFTA As Being Beneficial for U.S. Jobs," Christopher Swann points out that although he believes NAFTA has had a positive impact overall, American jobs have indeed been lost under the agreement. He discusses the need to reeducate and retrain workers so that they may return to the workforce in a more productive capacity instead of fruitlessly fighting to regain jobs already lost.

While Mexico has made many gains under NAFTA, the next article, "Mexico: Was NAFTA Worth It?" questions whether the country has paid too high a price for those benefits. The authors argue that NAFTA has not cured Mexico's economic ailments, as many of its proponents had promised, and consequently, many Mexicans have lost faith in the agreement.

In "What Happened When Two Countries Liberalized Trade? Pain, Then Gain," Virginia Postrel examines how NAFTA has impacted Canada. Initially, Postrel reports, Canada experienced job losses as companies formerly protected by tariffs found it difficult to compete with American firms. However, the increased competition eventually spurred Canadian companies to innovate and otherwise streamline and improve their operations, which in turn created huge gains in productivity and sparked impressive economic growth.

Integrating the North American Steel Market

By Dr. Hans Mueller
Steel Times International, January 2000

Examples of cities or countries banding together for greater economic strength go far back into history. In the Middle Ages a group of German, Scandinavian, and Polish cities succeeded for a surprisingly long period to pursue their common trade interests in a weakening political environment. Last century, several autonomous regions in Germany joined a customs union, as did Belgium, the Netherlands, and Luxembourg after World War II. A more decisive event was the formation in 1952 of the European Coal and Steel Community, an idealistic effort by six countries to banish future wars in Western Europe by putting two basic industries under common control. A few years later the European Economic Community was formed, which over time evolved into the 15-country European Union.

North American Free Trade Agreement

The North American Free Trade Agreement (NAFTA) between USA, Canada, and Mexico emerged in more recent times, in 1994.

In the Western Hemisphere, the most outstanding example of successful economic integration has been that of the USA, which by means of adaptable public and private institutions managed to create an efficient system of production, transportation, and communication spanning an enormous territorial expanse.

For a long time, relations between the USA and Mexico used to be anything but friendly. Foreign trade was limited to relatively few products, such as Mexican petroleum and U.S. cars and machinery, in addition to tourism and agricultural goods. In recent decades, a specialised *"maquiladora"* industry developed on the Mexican side of the border, where imported materials were assembled by cheap labour and shipped to the U.S. Most of these plants were operated by multinational corporations. In addition, companies from the U.S., Asia, and Europe were battling for shares of the Mexican automotive and appliance markets. With the North American Free Trade Agreement, the U.S. government sought to tie the Mexican economy closer to those of the USA and Canada.

Canada's geographic size results in most of its population being strung out in a narrow ribbon along its common border with the USA. Helped by a common language and tradition (with the exception of Quebec), Canada's economic activities have always been closely tied to those of its powerful neighbour to the south. In the Great Lakes region in particular, Canadian and U.S. industrial activity became highly interdependent and in 1989 this relationship was formalised by the U.S./Canadian Free Trade Agreement.

Growing to include Mexico in 1994 was not an easy fit. Mexico is not in the same league with the other two NAFTA members regarding economic infrastructure, educational standards, and administrative efficiency. It does not share a common language with them; its government institutions and legal system grew out of a different tradition. After NAFTA became effective, the Mexican Congress dragged its feet on measures to facilitate integration. Corruption among some politicians and government officials is not uncommon. Nevertheless, the country has enjoyed a high degree of political sta-

---

Creation of a free market with zero internal tariffs and a common external tariff must only be the first step in a continuing process of integration.

---

bility and, since its financial crisis in 1994/95, Mexico has experienced steady economic expansion. Few observers believe this will change after this year's elections, although many worry about the future growth rate of the USA, the destination of most of Mexico's manufacturing exports. Petroleum now accounts for less than 7 percent of total export value but as it brings in over 30 percent of public revenues, its higher global prices have been good news for the Mexican government.[1] In return, steel exports from the USA to its two NAFTA neighbours have risen steadily while exports to non-NAFTA countries have declined.

Ground Rules

European progress with economic integration has often been compared with the bicycle principle: "*if you stall, you fall.*" In other words, creation of a free market with zero internal tariffs and a common external tariff must only be the first step in a continuing process of integration or else it will eventually be undermined by inconsistent national rules and laws in such areas as trade (e.g., antidumping), competition, transportation, and communication.

This does not mean others must follow the European model of establishing at the start a set of far-reaching rules. The North American approach to basic changes is often more pragmatic in the hope that many problems can be worked out without resorting to formal guidance. NAFTA lacks a common policy-determining entity; it only has a 5-member dispute resolution panel to arbitrate disagreements, as e.g., on dumping decisions by national governments. Member countries remain free to conclude agreements with non-members, as Canada has done with Chile, and Mexico with the European Union. Moreover, private initiative can sometimes make up for the lack of appropriate rules. For example, several industry associations in the region have voluntarily begun to avoid antidumping action against other NAFTA steelmakers to prevent the re-segmentation of steel markets.

Relevant Data and Comparisons

In statistical terms, NAFTA and the European Union show some similarities. NAFTA's current population is about 400 million and its gross domestic product U.S.\$9,500 billion; the respective numbers for the EU are 375 million and U.S.\$8,500 billion.

As regards apparent steel consumption, it has been a close race. NAFTA pulled ahead of the EU in 1993–94 and again in 1996–98. According to the IISI, both regions registered 135Mt in 1999 but NAFTA will lag again in the current year, 136Mt vs. 139Mt. With respect to output, or shipments (where so reported), the 15-country EU industry has always been in the lead. For 1998, the numbers are approximately 122Mt for NAFTA and 137Mt for the EU. Both industries had to cope with a 50 percent increase in steel product imports in that year, which left NAFTA with a record 27Mt net-import balance and demolished the EU industry's traditionally significant steel trade surplus. 1999 should see some improvements in both instances due to defensive antidumping measures and a partial economic recovery in SE Asia.

Intraregional NAFTA Steel Trade

A large portion of exports by the three NAFTA steelmakers is shipped to customers in other member countries. If NAFTA were treated as a single political entity, this tonnage would be counted as internal commerce, as is steel trade between France and Germany in the case of the EU. Over 80 percent of U.S. exports are shipped to destinations in Canada and Mexico, most of it probably to U.S. companies operating there. More than 90 percent of Canadian and 75 percent of Mexican exports were bound for the other NAFTA members. More than half of U.S. imports from Mexico consist of semifinished products, whereas 60 percent of U.S. exports to Mexico are flat products. Steel trade between the U.S. and Canada covers the product spectrum more evenly.

Partial Solution to Antidumping

As noted, unlike the European institutions (ECSC, EEC, and EU), NAFTA did not formally put a stop to antidumping strife among member countries. Intra-regional steel trade has therefore been hampered by the effects of massive antidumping litigation in all three countries. The conflict began in 1992 with a volley of U.S. petitions filed against all major steel producers exporting flatrolled products to the U.S., including their Canadian and Mexican competitors. A partial U.S. victory on the eve of NAFTA's birth and subsequent retaliation by the Canadians and Mexicans against the U.S. aggressors caused some North American markets (notably those for plate and galvanised coils) to become fractured again. The inclusion of Mexico in the 1992/93 U.S. trade cases was all the more surprising as, at the time, the U.S. was running a large steel trade surplus with that country.

It took several years and an open rift with Canadian producers for the American Iron and Steel Institute (AISI) to realise the short-sightedness of a policy that supported the principle of NAFTA but at the same time foiled its success with antidumping action. The folly of this policy became all the more evident when multinational automotive and appliance firms responded to the promise of expanding markets with large investments in Mexico, which greatly increased the demand for imported steel, as local producers often could not meet the specifications for top-quality HR, CR, and coated products. Mexican imports from the EU, Brazil, and Japan increased considerably.

The change in the AISI's steel trade policy was also motivated by a sharp rise in North American steel imports from "non-market economies," Russia in particular, during the second half of the 1990s. A campaign was launched to woo Canadian and Mexican producers to help form a common front against the outside threat. The result was a barrage of antidumping petitions by the three industries against imports from Russia, Ukraine, and other CIS and East European countries. In return for this friendly co-operation, the integrated U.S. producers exempted Canada and Mexico in their most recent trade cases.

However, the same courtesy was not shown by other U.S. steel producer associations. The stainless producers targeted both Canada and Mexico in their recent attacks, while the pipe producers included Mexico in their petitions.

Nor do producers within Canada or Mexico always see eye to eye on trade policy. For example, Co-Steel, which operates wire rod plants in both the U.S. and Canada, has regularly joined U.S. petitioners when they filed against Canadian wire rod producers. And in Mexico, Ahmsa and Hylsa had no qualms about attacking Karmet, a sister company of Mexican slab producer Ispat Mexicana (*Imexsa*). A spokesman for Hylsa has also publicly supported the U.S. position that subsidies received by companies before they were privatised remain actionable. That dogma would make several Mexican producers—including Ahmsa, Imexsa, and Sicartsa—vulnerable to future attacks under foreign countervailing duty (anti-subsidy) laws.

Company Links Within NAFTA

EU member governments and leading banks used to put up stiff resistance to takeovers of major national steel producers by firms from other EU countries. But no longer. During the past few years the EU steel industry consolidated both within and across national boundaries to an extent where it has now become one of the most concentrated in the world. Will this yield greater efficiency, faster product innovation, and more customer satisfaction? Or will the long-term outcome be more bureaucracy, a sluggish response to change, and higher prices? Only time will tell.

The North American steel industry has remained at a very low level of concentration and there are as yet few major cross-border links within the NAFTA members. In the region, 26 companies now turn out less flatrolled carbon steel per year than do six producers in the EU. Only one company, Ispat, operates mills in the U.S., Canada, and Mexico (Inland, Sidbec-Dosco, and Imexsa, respectively).

On the U.S. side, there is the acquisition of Aceros Fortuna of Mexico by stainless long-product specialist Carpenter and the partial ownership by National Steel of a galvanising plant across the Canadian border (a JV with Dofasco). Canadian companies control several plants in the USA, such as the Gallatin HR sheet minimill (Dofasco/Co-Steel), wire rod producer Raritan (Co-Steel), a plate mill and plate processing centre (Ipsco, Atlantic Steel), several wire drawing mills (Ivaco), and 44 percent of Empire Specialty Steel by Atlas Specialty Steels. The Mexican Grupo Villacero, owner of Sicartsa, controls Border Steel, a small bar producer in the USA.[2]

In addition, there have been several downstream JVs linking U.S. and Mexican firms, such as Ryerson with Ahmsa (service centres), LTV with Imsa (steel buildings), LTV with Lagermex (processing), Hylsamex with Worthington (service centres), and Hylsa with AK Steel (joint sales).

Regarding performance in terms of output per steelmaking vessel, Canada is most efficient in the blast furnace–BOS route, but the least effective for electric arc steelmaking. Mexico is the predominant DRI producer, but the USA is by far the largest steel producer accounting for 76.7 percent of total output within NAFTA.

Conclusions

Should NAFTA succeed in putting an end to the intramural anti-dumping warfare, its steelmakers can probably count on more effective antidumping protection in future years than producers in the EU, where enforcement authorities tend to be less compliant with industry wishes.

With regards to the impact of economic integration on steel industry consolidation, it is somewhat early for a comparison, as NAFTA is still young and the European merger rush occurred quite recently. Nevertheless, unless the European giants themselves help expedite a merger movement in North America, there are few advance signals of industry consolidation in this market. Quite to the contrary; some U.S. producers are still expanding into additional product lines, a minimill entry may occur in Minnesota, and marginal or bankrupt mills can count on venturesome new owners or, since last year, federal government loan guarantees.

However, there is a likelihood that NAFTA steel producers might be able to observe some degree of pricing discipline due to various restraints on imports and the unifying effect of the recent battle against foreign competition. Needless to say, the success of such solidarity without consolidation will depend heavily on the strength of the market. Continued growth of consumption in the face of limited capacity expansion and subdued foreign competition may well push profits to a higher level than experienced even in the best years of the '90s. Whether the industry will manage to maintain closed ranks on the pricing front during a downturn is less certain.

References

1. Salvador Kalifa Assad, the Mexican economy on the threshold of the 21st century, ILAFA, 40 Congreso Latinoamericano de Siderurgia, September 1999, p 7–12.

2. For linkages between NAFTA and South American steelmakers see *Steel Times International*, November 1988, p 27.

Time to Bury the Hatchet

ECONOMIST, SEPTEMBER 16, 2004

For more than two decades, the export of Canadian wood to the United States has been the subject of a trade war. So it would be reckless to predict that peace is about to break out. Late last month, a ruling of a dispute panel of the North American Free Trade Agreement (NAFTA) demolished the United States' case for punitive tariffs, which is based on a claim that Canada's exports are subsidised. But Canadians are not celebrating yet.

The dispute is rooted in the two countries' different systems for managing forests. In the United States most are privately owned; timber prices are set by private contracts or auctions. In Canada, almost all forests are owned by the provinces, which grant long-term cutting rights and set stumpage rates (cutting fees) according to market conditions. To the American industry lobby, this government-led system with its "administratively set prices" confers subsidies.

In 2002, the United States Department of Commerce imposed countervailing and anti-dumping duties totalling 27 percent on Canadian imports. That forced Canada's lumber firms to shut some 50 mills and lay off thousands of workers. But despite the duties, Canada continues to supply a third of America's softwood market.

Canada denies subsidies are involved; it sees the duties as old-fashioned protection of a less efficient industry. In a series of rulings over the past two years, tribunals of the WTO and NAFTA have upheld Canada's argument. On August 31st, the NAFTA tribunal (with three American and two Canadian members) made a final, unanimous, ruling. Yet again, it rejected the claim that Canada's allegedly subsidised exports pose a "threat of material injury" to the American industry. It gave the United States International Trade Commission (ITC), a branch of the Department of Commerce, 10 days to accept this.

Jim Peterson, Canada's trade minister, welcomed the ruling as "an important first step" towards "long overdue" free trade in lumber in North America. He said that the next step is for the United States to revoke the duties, refund the C$3.4 billion ($2.4 billion) paid by Canadian firms, and then discuss ways to avoid further disputes.

Fat chance. On September 10th, the ITC said it accepted the NAFTA ruling. But only grudgingly: it lambasted the tribunal for "overstepping its authority . . . and committing legal error." That seems to open the way for an extraordinary challenge to the ruling. A final decision may rest with the Office of the United States Trade Representative, which is reviewing the case. It is being lobbied by the mighty producers' Coalition for Fair Lumber Imports—for years, a driving force behind the American duties. American consumer bodies, however, are delighted. The National Association of Home Builders, for instance, called the NAFTA panel's decision a "victory" for free trade that would help make homes more affordable.

The consumer lobby has gained strength in recent years. The Bush administration is keen on home ownership. American homes use much softwood; its price has risen by around a third since January. Recent hurricane damage in the south-east has jacked up demand for timber. But for now, the Commerce Department insists the duties will remain in place. Canadians are left to wonder whether their neighbours' rhetoric about free trade and the rule of law is just that.

NAFTA Contributing to Car Industry Success

By Katherine Yung
Detroit Free Press, December 24, 2003

On a former hacienda on the outskirts of this bustling border city [Tijuana, Mexico], out of sight from the tourist zone of boisterous bars and tacky souvenir shops, Toyota Motor Corp. is putting the finishing touches on its newest North American assembly plant.

A year from now, the Japanese automotive giant will employ 700 hourly workers in this gleaming white, $140-million factory, nestled under towering brown mountains.

The Tacoma pickup trucks built there will be Toyota's first vehicles made in Mexico. By launching production south of the border, Toyota will fill one of the last holes in the auto industry's increasingly unified production network stretching across North America.

"Now we look at Mexico, the U.S., and Canada as a more integrated market," said Dennis Cuneo, senior vice president of the Toyota North America Inc. subsidiary.

It's an outlook that owes much to the North American Free Trade Agreement, which is helping create a common market for the sale and production of new vehicles across the continent.

Shortly after NAFTA's 10th anniversary, the auto industry stands out as one of the major success stories of the controversial trade pact. "It's really completed the integration of the auto industry in North America," said Stephen Collins, president of the Automotive Trade Policy Council, which represents Detroit auto companies. "I call it a win-win-win. It's been a very successful agreement from our point of view."

Despite significantly increasing trade and deepening ties between the United States and Mexico, the agreement's reputation has been marred by the loss of more than a half-million U.S. manufacturing jobs and by its inability to raise living standards for millions of Mexicans.

But when it comes to automobiles, one of the biggest generators of international commerce, NAFTA's impact helps make the case for the merits of free trade.

The trade agreement has opened the Mexican market to imports from the United States and Canada, giving Mexican consumers greater choices in what they drive. It's allowed automakers the freedom to use their Mexican factories as they see fit, increasing their manufacturing efficiency.

And though many auto supplier jobs have moved south of the border, the worst fear about NAFTA hasn't been realized. Automakers haven't abandoned their U.S. assembly plants for new ones in Mexico at the expense of U.S. jobs.

"NAFTA's allowed for the integration of the Mexican auto industry with the U.S. auto industry," said G. Mustafa Mohatarem, chief economist at General Motors Corp. and head of its trade team.

> *"NAFTA's allowed for the integration of the Mexican auto industry with the U.S. auto industry."*
> —G. Mustafa Mohatarem, General Motors Corp.

Each year, cars, trucks, and their components account for a huge portion of the trade between the United States and its neighbors. Of the $258.4 billion in total U.S. exports to Canada and Mexico last year, 23 percent, or $59.6 billion, were motor vehicles and related parts. And these items accounted for nearly 30 percent of total U.S. imports from these countries.

Auto production has also served as one of the few economic bright spots for Mexico, which has seen many of its electronics and apparel factories move to China in search of cheaper labor.

Since NAFTA began, most of the industry's attention has focused on Mexico because the United States and Canada have long enjoyed the benefits of free trade in automobiles. Nearly three decades before NAFTA, the U.S.–Canadian Auto Pact of 1965 started dismantling tariffs and other trade barriers between the countries.

Mexico was a different story. In 1993, the year before NAFTA took effect, tariffs on cars and light trucks imported into the country stood at 20 percent. For every dollar's worth of imported vehicles, auto companies had to export $1.75. Onerous local content requirements and other regulations shielded the market from open competition.

NAFTA sought to change that. Tariffs have been gradually phased out and will be completely eliminated Jan. 1. For the first time, Mexicans will be able to cross into the United States, buy a car, and drive it back home without paying exorbitant fees.

Trade balancing rules and local content requirements are also disappearing. And auto companies will no longer need to build vehicles in Mexico to sell large numbers of them in the local market free of any duties.

"Since NAFTA, we have more products to give to the consumers at better prices," said Flavio Diaz Miron, Ford of Mexico's legal and government affairs director.

Mexicans have taken notice. Auto sales have shot up 66 percent since 1994, even with the country's peso crisis late that year. Today they hover just below 1 million vehicles per year and have outpaced sales gains in the United States and Canada by a wide margin over the last decade.

Automakers also rely more than ever on their factories south of the border. Mexico's share of total North American vehicle production has risen to 11 percent from 7 percent in 1993, said Carlos Gomes, senior economist at Scotia Economics in Toronto. Today nearly 10 percent of GM's total North American production comes from Mexico, up from 3.8 percent in 1993.

While Ford's Mexican production has declined since 1994, that trend isn't likely to continue. The automaker announced in October that it plans to double capacity at its Hermosillo plant to build the Futura, a new midsize sedan.

NAFTA's Impacts on U.S. Agriculture: Trade & Beyond

By Steven Zahniser
Agricultural Outlook, October 2002

NAFTA, the North American Free Trade Agreement, has generally benefited U.S. agriculture and related industries. U.S. agricultural trade with Canada and Mexico more than doubled during the
1990s, a development to which NAFTA contributed. Moreover, the
agreement has established rules and institutions that mitigate
potential trade frictions, promote foreign direct investment, and
facilitate public discourse about environmental issues. Thus,
NAFTA's effects on agriculture should be assessed not only in terms
of trade impacts, but also for the trade, investment, and institutional reforms resulting from its implementation.

The adjustment to freer trade in North America has been relatively smooth. Most U.S. barriers to Canadian and Mexican exports
were low prior to NAFTA, and dismantling of tariffs under the
agreement is in general proceeding gradually. However, the U.S.
dollar has tended to appreciate in real terms against the Canadian
dollar since 1992. While this development is not the result of
NAFTA, it has made U.S. farm exports more expensive to Canadian
customers while making imports more affordable to U.S. consumers.
In contrast, the real value of the U.S. dollar in Mexican *pesos* has
tended to decline in recent years, gradually reversing the precipi-
tous drop in the *peso's* value that occurred in late 1994 and early
1995. This increase in value of the *peso* has worked to the advantage
of U.S. exports to Mexico.

NAFTA Has Increased Trade of Some Products

NAFTA, which took effect January 1, 1994, provides for the progressive dismantling of most barriers to trade and investment
among Canada, Mexico, and the U.S. over the 14-year period ending
January 1, 2008. The agreement incorporates the Canada–U.S. Free
Trade Agreement (CFTA), whose implementation was completed on
January 1, 1998. Although NAFTA's transition is still in progress,
tariff elimination for agricultural products is nearly complete. For
this reason, NAFTA's influence on U.S. agriculture to date should
provide a good indication of the agreement's long-term impacts.

Article from *Agricultural Outlook*, October 2002, U.S. Dept. of Agriculture, Economic Research
Service. Reprinted with permission.

U.S. agricultural trade with Canada and Mexico has continued on an upward trend since NAFTA's implementation. While only a portion of this increase can be attributed solely to the agreement, NAFTA has allowed competitive market forces to play a more dominant role in determining agricultural trade flows among the three countries. The agreement has facilitated a reorientation of U.S. agricultural trade in which U.S. exporters and importers put greater focus on the NAFTA region. In 2001, 29 percent of U.S. agricultural exports were destined for either Canada or Mexico, and the two countries supplied 38 percent of U.S. agricultural imports. In 1990, these shares were 17 percent and 25 percent, respectively.

To examine NAFTA's trade impact, USDA's Economic Research Service estimated the trade changes resulting from CFTA and NAFTA for 38 commodities or commodity groupings, isolating the agreements' influence from population growth, changes in macroeconomic performance and exchange rates, unusual weather patterns, and other factors. For commodities subject to quotas or other quantitative restrictions before CFTA and NAFTA, the volume of trade during 1994–2000 was compared with previously allowed quantities. This assumed no over-quota trading except where analysts determined that previous limits were not enforced. For commodities subject to tariffs prior to CFTA and NAFTA, economic models and assessments by commodity trade specialists were used to estimate the impact of tariff changes.

U.S. agricultural trade with Canada and Mexico has continued on an upward trend since NAFTA's implementation.

For most commodities, NAFTA's trade effect has been relatively minor, generating a small increase in U.S. exports to or imports from Canada or Mexico over what would have occurred without the agreement. For a handful of commodities, NAFTA's impact has been larger, with an increase of 15 percent or more in trade attributable to the agreement. This increase is particularly noticeable for products whose trade was severely restricted prior to CFTA and NAFTA.

U.S.–Canada beef trade has expanded substantially from the elimination of quantitative restrictions formerly imposed by both countries. In fact, U.S. beef exports to Canada may be twice as high as without CFTA and NAFTA. In addition, NAFTA tariff reductions have provided a moderate boost to U.S. beef exports to Mexico. Continued economic growth in Mexico should strengthen demand for this high-value product.

Because of animal health considerations, North American hog trade consists almost entirely of Canadian exports to the U.S. and U.S. exports to Mexico. Canadian hog exports to the U.S. increased from about 900,000 head in 1994 to 5.3 million head in 2001, due largely to Canada's elimination of grain transport and other agricultural subsidies, rather than to CFTA or NAFTA. Removal of

U.S. Ag Trade With Canada Has Continued to Climb Since NAFTA. . .

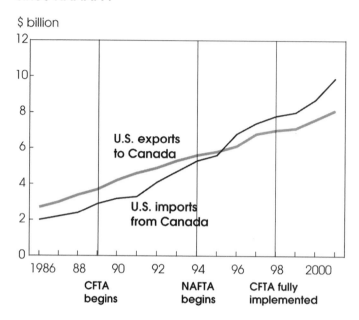

. . .As Has U.S. Ag Trade With Mexico

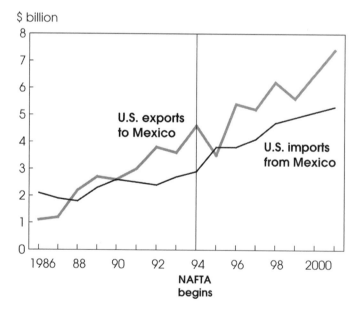

CFTA = Canada-U.S. Free Trade Agreement. NAFTA = North American Free Trade Agreement.

Economic Research Service, USDA

subsidy assistance to grain and hog producers, in particular, provided a strong incentive for the local use of grain in livestock production, and it helped bring about an end to U.S. countervailing
duties on Canadian hogs. U.S. hog exports to Mexico currently face
a duty of 35.1 cents per kilogram, the result of a Mexican antidumping investigation in 1998 and 1999.

CFTA and NAFTA have had a small, positive impact on U.S.
pork and poultry meat exports to Canada and Mexico, but the
influence of other factors has been more powerful. Sustained economic growth in Mexico during the late 1990s boosted demand for
U.S. pork and poultry, and both Canada and Mexico have shown
flexibility in their application of quantitative restrictions on U.S.
poultry.

Mexico's import policy toward U.S. corn is more open than
required by NAFTA, and a series of droughts limited Mexican corn
production in past years. U.S. corn exports to Mexico in 2001 were
more than three times their average volume during 1990–93.
Although Mexico eliminated its seasonal tariff on U.S. sorghum as
part of NAFTA, some Mexican livestock producers switched from
sorghum to corn feed due to increased availability of U.S. corn.
Still, sorghum is one of the major U.S. agricultural exports to Mexico.

The gradual elimination of tariffs on U.S.–Canada corn trade has
facilitated increased volumes of trade in years when bad weather
severely damaged the crop in one country but not the other. A
prominent example of this occurred in 2001, when a drought in
Canada led to the importation of 3 million metric tons (mt) of U.S.
corn, compared with an annual average of just 890,000 mt during
1990–2000.

CFTA and NAFTA also gradually did away with tariffs on U.S.–
Canada wheat trade. Although this reform has increased U.S.
wheat *imports* from Canada by a large amount, its impact on U.S.
wheat *exports* to Canada is negligible, reflecting both Canada's historic strength in wheat production and the long-term impact of
Canada's various regulatory actions.

Canada and the U.S. continue to spar over the activities of the
Canadian Wheat Board (CWB), and in February 2002, the Office of
the U.S. Trade Representative (USTR) completed a Section 301
investigation of this subject, in which it concluded that the CWB
had "taken sales" from U.S. wheat farmers. In its finding, USTR
outlined several measures that it would take to "level the playing
field" for U.S. farmers, including the exploration of a possible dispute settlement case against the CWB in the World Trade Organization. Section 301 of the Trade Act of 1974, as amended,
authorizes the federal government to impose trade sanctions
against foreign countries under certain conditions, including the
violation of a trade agreement with the U.S. and the maintenance
of "unjustifiable, unreasonable, or discriminatory" policies that

restrict U.S. commerce. Section 301 investigations are conducted by USTR and may be initiated in response to a petition from an interested party or self-initiated by USTR.

The U.S. is currently the predominant foreign supplier of rice to Mexico, due largely to Mexico's strict phytosanitary standards which the U.S. meets but other major exporters do not. Should Asian rice exporters satisfactorily meet these standards, the U.S. tariff advantage under NAFTA would become extremely important to U.S. rice exporters. Rough rice accounts for the bulk of Mexico's rice imports. Currently, no major Asian rice producer allows this product to be exported, in an effort to preserve jobs associated with rice processing. Long grain milled rice from the U.S. has been subject to Mexican antidumping duties of up to 10.18 percent since June 2002. Shipments of this product make up about 10 percent of U.S. rice exports to Mexico.

NAFTA's impact on U.S.–Canada oilseed trade differs substantially from its impact on U.S.–Mexico trade in oilseeds. CFTA and NAFTA have increased two-way trade between Canada and the U.S. in processed oilseed products, particularly vegetable oil. In contrast, NAFTA has boosted U.S. soybean exports to Mexico, as expansion of the Mexican livestock industry has increased the demand for vegetable meal, which Mexico satisfies by crushing imported oilseeds.

Creation of a tariff-rate quota (TRQ) for raw peanuts from Mexico has enabled that country to export substantial quantities of this product to the U.S. for the first time. In the last several years, Mexico also has begun to export peanut butter and paste to the U.S., but these products make up only a small proportion of U.S. consumption. U.S. imports of Canadian peanut butter are restricted by a TRQ, one of the few remaining tariff barriers between the U.S. and Canada.

To qualify for NAFTA tariff reductions, textiles and apparel traded among the NAFTA countries must be made from yarn and fiber produced by a NAFTA member. These provisions have enabled the U.S. textile and apparel industries to integrate more closely with their Canadian and Mexican counterparts. As part of this process, U.S. cotton exports to Canada and Mexico more than doubled in volume between 1993 and 2000, while apparel imports from Mexico and other countries increased.

NAFTA is gradually expanding duty-free quotas for U.S.–Mexico sugar trade, as the two countries move toward free trade in this commodity starting in fiscal year (FY) 2008. The formula for the quota on Mexican shipments to the U.S. is based on the difference between Mexico's projected production and projected domestic consumption, including an allowance for consumption of high-fructose corn syrup. As the quotas have expanded, Mexico's access to the U.S. sugar market has climbed from 7,258 mt prior to NAFTA to 116,000 mt in FY 2001. These imports, along with low world prices for sugar, pose challenges for the U.S. sugar support program.

CFTA and NAFTA have affected some aspects of North American tomato trade, but other factors have played a more prominent role. A price-floor agreement among principal Mexican and U.S. growers secured the suspension of U.S. antidumping duties on fresh tomatoes from Mexico from 1996 to 2002. The price-floor agreement ended in August 2002, after Mexican growers submitted written notice of their withdrawal, and the antidumping duties, which were based on a preliminary U.S. investigation, have since been imposed.

Increasing U.S. demand for high-quality tomatoes and the relative strength of the U.S. dollar have fostered the emergence of sizable Canadian exports of hydroponic tomatoes to the U.S. Between 1990 and 2000, Canadian exports of fresh or chilled tomatoes to the U.S. expanded from about 3,000 mt to more than 101,000 mt. In 2001, U.S. tomato growers initiated an antidumping case against Canadian producers of greenhouse tomatoes, and a Canadian trade organization filed a similar suit concerning fresh tomatoes from the U.S. Neither case resulted in the imposition of antidumping duties.

U.S. imports of processed tomatoes from Mexico have shifted in recent years from primarily tomato paste to increasing quantities of tomato juice and sauce, a change that is partially due to NAFTA tariff changes. As part of NAFTA, the U.S. immediately eliminated its tariff on Mexican tomato juice and ketchup in 1994, and is gradually phasing out its tariffs on other processed tomato products from Mexico. Tariff elimination under CFTA and NAFTA also has boosted U.S. tomato sauce exports to Canada.

CFTA and NAFTA also have influenced North American potato trade. Elimination of U.S. tariffs on fresh potatoes from Canada has provided a moderate boost to Canadian fresh potato exports to the U.S. But an expansion in Canadian potato production and processing and the strong U.S. dollar have played even greater roles in the growth of Canadian exports of frozen french fries to the U.S. Through Mexico's establishment of a transitional TRQ with a low preferential tariff for processed potatoes from the U.S., NAFTA has had a large, positive impact on U.S. processed potato exports to Mexico, particularly frozen french fries.

North American fruit trade provides many examples of NAFTA's impacts. U.S. grape and pear exports to Mexico expanded with the end of Mexican import licensing on grapes and the elimination of Mexico's tariff on U.S. pears, both the result of NAFTA. Mexico's transitional TRQ for fresh apples from the U.S. has had a large, positive impact on U.S. apple exports to Mexico, but a minimum-price arrangement forged by the Mexican government and the U.S. apple industry in order to suspend Mexican antidumping duties has worked to limit this trade. On the U.S. import side, NAFTA tariff reductions have provided a moderate stimulus to

Mexican shipments of cantaloupes to the U.S. These shipments had decreased during the mid-1990s due to weather-related damage in some producing areas in Mexico.

NAFTA Has Facilitated Investment & Aggregate Employment

NAFTA's rules concerning foreign direct investment (FDI) strengthen the rights of foreign investors to retain profits and returns from their initial capital investments. The combination of trade liberalization and investment reform has stimulated FDI in the North American food processing industry, with firms in each NAFTA country providing substantial investment capital.

The stock of U.S. direct investment in the Mexican food processing industry has increased by about two-thirds since NAFTA's implementation, reaching $3.8 billion in 1999. Much of this investment is concentrated in highly processed products such as pasta, confectionery items, and canned and frozen meats. Similarly, under CFTA and NAFTA, U.S. FDI in the Canadian food processing industry expanded from $1.8 billion in 1989 to $5.8 billion in 1999. But

---

NAFTA has likely had a small, positive influence on the overall level of U.S. agricultural employment.

---

unlike FDI in Mexico, U.S. FDI in Canada is geared more towards the handling and processing of grains.

Mexican firms also increased their investments in U.S. food companies. In 1999, Mexican FDI in the U.S. processed food industry equaled $1 billion, compared with just $306 million in 1997. Mexican companies own U.S.–based firms engaged in bread baking, tortilla making, corn milling, and the manufacture of Mexican-style food products, just to name a few examples.

In contrast, the stock of Canadian direct investment in the U.S. processed food industry dropped from $6.7 billion in 1998 to about $1.0 billion in 1999, following the liquidation of a major company's assets. This reduction is a sharp departure from the first several years of NAFTA, when Canadian FDI in the U.S. processed food industry grew from $5.1 billion in 1993 to $7.6 billion in 1997, exceeding the U.S. presence in Canada.

By increasing opportunities for U.S. exports and encouraging a more efficient allocation of economic resources, NAFTA has likely had a small, positive influence on the overall level of U.S. agricultural employment. But this impact is difficult to detect, in part because many aspects of U.S. agricultural production are capital intensive, and in part because factors other than NAFTA have driven many of the employment changes. Employment in crop production has changed very little overall since NAFTA's implementation, while employment in livestock production has decreased, reflecting technological change and consolidation in the hog industry and drought and poor range conditions in the cattle industry.

Two manufacturing sectors related to agriculture—textiles and apparel—have experienced a definite decline in employment since implementation of NAFTA. The reduction began in the 1970s and most likely would have continued in NAFTA's absence. By encouraging the development of a more integrated textile and apparel industry within North America, the agreement has expanded textile and apparel trade among the NAFTA countries and increased productivity in the U.S. textile and apparel sectors. But this development has been accompanied by further reductions in U.S. textile and apparel employment.

Resolving Trade Frictions in the NAFTA Era

Sanitary and phytosanitary measures. By "locking in" key trade and investment reforms, the agricultural sectors and governments of NAFTA partners have been able to devote greater attention to resolving conflicts related to sanitary and phytosanitary (SPS) measures. Some initiatives on these measures have taken place within the trilateral NAFTA Committee on SPS Measures. In addition, producers in each NAFTA country have worked to formulate and meet higher quality standards.

Inspection and approval of product quality at the regional level, and in some instances at the level of individual producers, have opened the door to new markets across international borders. Resulting developments include:

- imports of avocados to the U.S. from certain approved growers in the Mexican state of Michoacán;

- U.S. recognition of the Mexican states of Sonora and Yucatan as having a low risk of transmitting hog cholera;

- Mexico's lifting of its ban on citrus from Arizona and certain producing areas in Texas that are not regulated for fruit fly; and

- continuing efforts to design and implement a satisfactory inspection process for U.S. apple exports to Mexico.

Trade remedies. Trade growth and liberalization can generate conflicts. Agricultural producers in each NAFTA country have been involved in a number of disputes, many of which concern antidumping and countervailing-duty measures against imports regarded as harmful to domestic industry. NAFTA arbitration panels currently are looking at two agricultural cases concerning Final Antidumping Duty Determinations by Mexico. One panel is addressing U.S. exports to Mexico of high-fructose corn syrup; the other is dealing with U.S. exports of bovine carcasses. Previous

NAFTA panels have issued rulings in cases involving U.S. exports of refined sugar to Canada, Canadian exports of live swine to the U.S., and Mexican exports of fresh cut flowers to the U.S.

Transportation issues. Mexico successfully brought a case before a NAFTA arbitration panel concerning U.S. delays in implementing the agreement's provisions for cross-border trucking. In response, the U.S. is establishing a safety inspection and certification system for Mexican trucks entering the U.S. to be administered by the U.S. Department of Transportation's Federal Motor Carrier Safety Administration. This will allow Mexican trucks to continue to U.S. destinations without reloading their goods to U.S. trucks, which has been a bottleneck hampering trade and causing congestion. Several studies have quantified total delay costs along the entire U.S.–Mexico border, with the most recent comprehensive study placing these costs at $77.4 million in 1999. This estimate would have been even higher if increases in air pollution associated with traffic congestion at the borders had been taken into account.

NAFTA appears to have a combination of positive and negative environmental effects.

Further development of the Mexican transportation system will influence the modes of transportation that are used in U.S.–Mexico agricultural trade. With continuing integration of U.S. and Mexican railway systems, intermodal rail (truck-rail-truck) may handle increased traffic in containerized grains. Improvements in the Mexican Port of Veracruz should increase the competitiveness of ocean grain shipping from U.S. ports along the Gulf Coast. But improvements in Mexican ports may also lower transportation costs for U.S. competitors.

Environmental concerns. NAFTA appears to have a combination of positive and negative environmental effects, as producers select alternative techniques of production, increase or decrease the scale of production, and modify the crop and animal composition of their activities in response to changing economic incentives. The notion that NAFTA has encouraged a general weakening of environmental quality and protection has been refuted by a comparative study in 2000 of the environmental regulations of border and nonborder states.

Among NAFTA's innovations was the creation of the North American Commission for Environmental Cooperation (CEC), which promotes environmental objectives and provides opportunities for environmental organizations and other stakeholders to voice their concerns. Several public symposia have been held under the auspices of the CEC. By bringing environmental concerns before policymakers, these gatherings have facilitated coordination of trade and environmental policies and lessened potential conflicts.

Formal NAFTA mechanisms represent only a small part of the dispute resolution process. Most disputes are addressed in earlier stages through governmental consultations and negotiations. The private sector also has begun to play a larger role in dispute resolution. For example, in two disputes over grapes and cattle, producer groups in Mexico and the U.S. worked jointly to resolve regulatory incompatibilities that were at the root of the disagreement.

By facilitating increased trade and investment among Canada, Mexico, and the U.S., NAFTA is enabling agricultural producers throughout North America to benefit more fully from their relative strengths and to respond more efficiently to changing economic conditions. Each NAFTA country has participated in the expanded agricultural trade and FDI fostered by the agreement. Moreover, the agreement has been accompanied by substantial improvements in the North American transportation system and in the institutional capacity of the NAFTA governments to facilitate agricultural trade, resolve trade disputes, and cooperate on environmental issues. Together, these developments can lead to a more prosperous, more integrated North American economy.

NAFTA Sprouts Mexico Woe

By Hugh Dellios
Chicago Tribune, January 10, 2003

Heaving bales of winter cornstalk feed into pens full of grunting hogs, the dozen hired hands at El Molino farm worry that they won't be around to tackle these chores a year from now.

Although they work for a farmer who has modernized his operation and turned it organic, many of the farmhands fear they might have to search for the same type of work north of the border—illegally.

Across the Mexican countryside, such worries have turned into threats of violence over the Jan. 1 lifting of tariffs on the import of agricultural products between the United States and Mexico in the second phase of the 9-year-old North American Free Trade Agreement.

Farmers have threatened to block U.S.–Mexico border crossings; some stormed the chambers of Mexico's Congress on horseback last month. They are demanding that their government renegotiate the accord or provide compensation for what is expected to be a flood of U.S. pork, chicken, and other farm products across the border.

While Mexican officials say NAFTA has helped their country overall, rural Mexicans remained at a strict disadvantage.

Mexico's admitted failure to make expected advances to level the playing field with the U.S. and Canada is part of the problem. But the farmers also complain that they can't compete with the $7 billion a year in federal subsidies that they say allow U.S. farmers to undersell them and dominate markets.

"They talk about a free trade treaty, but it's better to call it a treaty of trade from there to here," said Jorge Angel Ozuna, coordinator of meat-product markets for the Jalisco state government. "Until now, we are at a great disadvantage."

The timing of the tariff elimination and the resulting protests put President Vicente Fox in a bind ahead of midterm elections for Congress, which many see as a referendum on his first three years in office.

In response, his administration has agreed to formal negotiations with representatives from across the rural and farming sectors. The participants hope to reach an accord that will bring help to Mexico's long-neglected agricultural industry.

"The countryside continues deteriorating," said Guadalupe Martinez Cruz, an opposition senator who represents farmers. "If we don't attack the farm problem, we're going to have more hot spots, because there's a lack of jobs, a lack of economic circulation, regional development, competition with our commercial partners abroad and even inside our own country."

"You Have to Go North"

Around Alvaro Obregon in Michoacán state, where 2.5 million residents already work in the United States, officials say the continuing loss of rural jobs inevitably will result in more illegal immigration to the U.S.

"These days, you have to go north. There's nothing to do here," said Manuel Lopez, 67, who hired two farmhands to replace his two U.S.–bound sons in the cornfields this season.

> "If we don't attack the farm problem, we're going to have more hot spots."
> —Guadalupe Martinez Cruz, a Mexican senator

Martinez and others have demanded a NAFTA compensation fund to benefit the farmers. A few weeks ago, Fox's government agreed to reinstitute crop subsidies for Mexican farmers at a total of $10 billion over a number of years.

All sides agree Mexican farmers need more government loans and credits, better transportation to market, improved irrigation technology, better storage methods, clearer land titles, and, in some cases, job prospects away from the farms. They also complain that Mexico's failure to establish national product standards has cost farmers the credibility needed to compete in U.S. markets.

While broaching the problems at least twice with President Bush, Fox has made it clear that one tactic he won't pursue is trying to reopen the NAFTA accords to get a better deal.

"It doesn't make sense to get ourselves involved in a fight that will cost us a lot in exchange for very little," Fox told farm producers last month.

"The solution is in being competitive and productive, and we have promised you this and we are taking the pertinent measures," he added.

NAFTA has benefited Mexico in many ways.

Twenty percent of Mexico's current gross domestic product is now attributable to NAFTA reforms, according to figures from the U.S. Embassy.

Agricultural exports to the U.S. have doubled to $6.7 billion since 1993, and bilateral trade increased by 115 percent, according to the Mexican Ministry of Economy.

Tough Times on Hog Farms

While the free-trade reforms have boosted exports of mangoes, bananas, watermelon, and cantaloupe to U.S. consumers, there have been hard times for other producers, especially hog farmers.

The import of U.S. pork products has doubled during the past 10 years, and a full third of Mexican hog producers have left the business, according to the Mexican Hog Farmers Association.

Matters could get even worse now that the 2.5 percent tariff on pork imports has been removed. The chicken industry, which was protected by a 49 percent tariff, could be hurt even more.

In a move scheduled when NAFTA was signed in 1993, the new rules removed customs duties on about 80 agricultural products. Remaining tariffs—on corn, beans, and powdered milk—will be lifted in 2008.

U.S. officials insist that it is Mexican industry problems more than U.S. farm subsidies that still may be tilting the playing field toward the north.

On a recent trade visit to Mexico, Jill Appell, a board member for the National Pork Producers Council and a family pork farmer from Altona, Ill., said that smaller U.S. pork producers are going through the same kinds of problems as their Mexican counterparts.

She said the number of pork farmers in the U.S. has shrunk from 221,000 in 1993 to 81,000 today and they are only indirectly subsidized through federal payments to feed grain growers.

NAFTA "is an excuse," Appell said about Mexico's complaints. "Their problem is partly that they're not efficient. They have disease problems and their product is not consistent, and so their market is more restrictive."

Yet Mario Ortiz Aguilar, owner of El Molino farm in Alvaro Obregon, said he had invested in more modern technology during the last decade and instituted a more disease-resistant operation by using organic methods.

Still, it did not help him market his pork to the United States, which would not certify hog products for import from his Michoacán region because of wider sanitation concerns.

"I'm getting squeezed," Ortiz said. "I just can't win."

Symposium: Has NAFTA Been a Good Deal for the Average Worker?

By Daniel T. Griswold and William R. Hawkins
Insight on the News, January 21, 2003

YES: NAFTA has led to more and better jobs, while bringing political reforms to Mexico.
By Daniel T. Griswold

Ten years ago, on Dec. 17, 1992, leaders of the United States, Canada, and Mexico signed the historic North American Free Trade Agreement (NAFTA). While each of the leaders—President George H. W. Bush of the United States, President Carlos Salinas of Mexico, and Prime Minister Brian Mulroney of Canada—suffered less-than-triumphal exits from office, they all can rightly claim credit for the success of NAFTA as a pioneering policy initiative.

Although NAFTA remains a lightning rod for critics of free trade—and will be debated anew as Congress soon considers a free trade agreement with Chile—by any measure it has been a public-policy success. As a trade agreement, it delivered its principal objective of more trade. Since 1993, the value of two-way U.S. trade with Mexico has almost tripled, from $81 billion to $232 billion, growing twice as fast as U.S. trade with the rest of the world. Canada and Mexico now are the United States' No. 1 and No. 2 trading partners respectively, with Japan a distant third.

One reason NAFTA remains controversial is that advocates and opponents alike were guilty of exaggerating its potential impact. Advocates claimed it would create hundreds of thousands of jobs in the U.S. economy from a dramatic rise in exports; opponents claimed it would destroy far more jobs from a flood of imports entering the United States and a stampede of U.S. companies moving to Mexico to take advantage of cheap wages. As H. Ross Perot famously predicted during the third presidential debate in 1992, "You're going to hear a giant sucking sound of jobs being pulled out of this country."

In reality, NAFTA had little impact on the U.S. economy. America's gross domestic product at the time was almost 20 times larger than that of Mexico, and U.S. tariffs against Mexican goods already averaged a low 2 percent. The agreement really was about institutionalizing Mexico's economic reform.

For the United States, NAFTA always had been more about foreign policy than the domestic economy. Its biggest dividend was to institutionalize our southern neighbor's turn away from centralized protection and toward decentralized, democratic capitalism. By that measure, NAFTA has been a spectacular success. In the decade since signing NAFTA, Mexico has continued along the road of economic and political reform. It successfully has decoupled its economy from the old boom-and-bust, high-inflation, debt-ridden model that characterized it and much of Latin America until the 1980s. When Mexico's old protectionist model crashed and burned in the debt crisis of 1982, it took seven years to regain its international credit rating and for U.S. exports to Mexico to regain their precrisis level. After the peso crisis of 1994–95, it took Mexico only seven months to regain its credit rating and 17 months for U.S. exports to Mexico to recover. In 2000, Mexico avoided an election-cycle economic crisis for the first time since the 1970s. Today, Mexico and Chile are the two most stable and dynamic major economies in Latin America—and the two that have reformed most aggressively.

In the decade since signing NAFTA, Mexico has continued along the road of economic and political reform.

Just as importantly, the economic competition and decentralization embodied in NAFTA encouraged more political competition in Mexico. It broke the economic grip of the dominant Institutional Revolutionary Party (PRI) for most of the last century. It is no mere coincidence that within seven years of NAFTA's implementation, Mexicans were able to elect opposition-party candidate Vicente Fox as president after 71 years of the PRI's one-party rule. Alejandro Junco, publisher of the opposition newspaper *Reforma*, noted after the PRI's historic defeat, "As the years have passed, and with international mechanisms like NAFTA, the government doesn't control the newsprint, they don't have the monopoly on telecommunications, there's a consciousness among citizens that the president can't control everybody."

On this 10th anniversary of the NAFTA signing, let's return to the battlefield where it originally was debated—that of jobs, foreign investment, and the American "industrial base." But even on the terms of the opponents, it is difficult to find any evidence of a "giant sucking sound" of jobs, investment, and manufacturing capacity heading south.

American jobs. Trade is not about more jobs or fewer jobs; it's about better jobs, and NAFTA is no exception. Of course increased competition from Mexico led to the closure of some U.S. factories that had been competing directly with Mexican-based producers. Those closures have allowed resources to shift to those areas where U.S. producers enjoy a relatively large advantage in efficiency. That's the whole idea of trade: We increase production in those areas where we are more efficient and reduce production where we are less efficient. The result is a shift to better-paying jobs. Meanwhile, the overall level of employment is determined by such macroeconomic factors as monetary policy, labor-market regulations, and the business cycle.

After the enactment of NAFTA on Jan. 1, 1994, the U.S. economy continued to create millions of jobs throughout the 1990s. Civilian employment in the U.S. economy grew from 120.3 million in 1993

The North American Free Trade Agreement (NAFTA)

WORLD ALMANAC & BOOK OF FACTS, 2004

NAFTA, a comprehensive plan for free trade between the U.S., Canada, and Mexico, took effect Jan. 1, 1994. Major provisions are:

Agriculture—Tariffs on all farm products are to be eliminated over 15 years. Domestic price-support systems may continue provided they do not distort trade.

Automobiles—By 2003, at least 62.5 percent of an automobile's value must have been produced in North America for it to qualify for duty-free status. Tariffs are to be phased out over 10 years.

Banking—U.S. and Canadian banks may acquire Mexican commercial banks accounting for as much as 8 percent of the industry's capital. All limits on ownership end in 2004.

Disputes—Special judges have jurisdiction to resolve disagreements within strict timetables.

Energy—Mexico continues to bar foreign ownership of its oil fields but, starting in 2004, U.S. and Canadian companies can bid on contracts offered by Mexican oil and electricity monopolies.

Environment—The trade agreement cannot be used to overrule national and state environmental, health, or safety laws.

Immigration—All three countries must ease restrictions on the movement of business executives and professionals.

Jobs—Barriers to limit Mexican migration to U.S. remain.

Patent and copyright protection—Mexico strengthened its laws providing protection to intellectual property.

Tariffs—Tariffs on 10,000 customs goods are to be eliminated over 15 years. One-half of U.S. exports to Mexico are to be considered duty-free within five years.

Textiles—A "rule of origin" provision requires most garments to be made from yarn and fabric that have been produced in North America. Most tariffs are being phased out over five years.

Trucking—Trucks were to have free access on crossborder routes and throughout the three countries by 1999, but the U.S. continued to impose restrictions on Mexican trucks. In 2001, an arbitration panel ruled that the U.S. restrictions were in violation of NAFTA. Pres. Bush in Nov. 2002 eased restrictions on Mexican trucks entering the U.S.

---

to 135.1 million in 2001, an increase of almost 2 million jobs per year. The unemployment rate fell steadily after the enactment of NAFTA, from an average of 6.9 percent in 1993 to less than 4 percent in 2000. The unemployment rate jumped to 6 percent in 2002, but that was because of the recent and relatively mild recession of 2001—a recession brought on not by NAFTA but by rising interest rates and energy prices, and a falling stock market.

> *U.S. investment in Mexico is modest compared with what we invest domestically.*

Opponents allege that, while the number of jobs may have increased, real wages have fallen since the passage of NAFTA. In Mexico, the charge rings half true. The peso crisis of 1994–95 caused real wages to drop, but that crisis really was the last gasp of the old order, not the fault of NAFTA. And since then, real wages in Mexico have recovered. In the United States, the charge is wholly false. In fact, in the last half of the 1990s, real compensation rose at a healthy pace up and down the income scale. Even through the recent recession, real wages have kept rising because of surprisingly strong productivity growth.

Foreign investment. Despite dire predictions, NAFTA did not cause an exodus of manufacturing investment to Mexico. Yes, U.S. investment in Mexico did increase after NAFTA, along with trade, but it remains a trickle compared with annual investment in the domestic U.S. economy. Lower wages are not the only reason a U.S. company invests abroad. Foreign direct investment seeks wealthy consumers, modern infrastructure, open trade, the rule of law, protected property rights, and an educated and productive workforce. For all those reasons, U.S. companies invest far more in other advanced, high-wage, high-standard economies than they do in less-developed countries such as Mexico.

U.S. investment in Mexico is modest compared with what we invest domestically. In the eight years after the implementation of NAFTA, from 1994 through 2001, U.S. manufacturing companies invested an average of $2.2 billion a year in factories in Mexico. That is a mere 1 percent of the $200 billion invested in manufacturing each year in the domestic U.S. economy. The small outflow of direct manufacturing investment to Mexico has been overwhelmed by the net inflow of such investment from the rest of the world—an average of $16 billion a year since 1994, most of it from Europe and Japan. At the end of 2001, the stock of U.S. direct manufacturing investment in Mexico was $19.7 billion—less than one-tenth the stock of U.S. investment in Europe.

U.S. manufacturing. Nowhere were the predictions about NAFTA more apocalyptic than in regard to manufacturing. Perot accused NAFTA of "deindustrializing our country," and Rep. David Bonior, the now-soon-to-be ex-congressman and Democratic whip from Michigan, predicted flatly that NAFTA "will destroy the auto industry."

Since the implementation of NAFTA, those predictions have become laughable. Since 1994, manufacturing output in the United States as measured by the U.S. Federal Reserve Board rose by one-third. Output of motor vehicles and parts rose by 30 percent. In fact, in the eight years after NAFTA, manufacturing output in the United States rose at an annual average rate of 3.7 percent—50 percent faster than during the eight years before enactment of NAFTA. Of course this is not an argument that NAFTA was the primary cause of the acceleration in manufacturing output, but it does knock the wind out of the myth that NAFTA somehow has caused the "deindustrialization" of the United States.

It is true that the number of Americans employed in manufacturing has taken a hit in recent years, but this cannot in any plausible way be blamed on NAFTA. In fact, the number of Americans employed in manufacturing grew by 707,000 in the first four years of NAFTA, from January 1994 to January 1998. The decline in manufacturing jobs since has not been because those jobs have gone to Mexico but because of: 1) collapsing demand for U.S. exports due to the East Asian financial meltdown in 1997–98; 2) the United States' own domestic slowdown in demand due to the 2001 recession; and 3) the ongoing dramatic improvement in manufacturing productivity, fueled by information technology and increased global competition, that has allowed American factories to produce more widgets with fewer workers.

By every reasonable measure, NAFTA has been a public-policy success in the decade since it was signed. It has deepened and institutionalized Mexico's drive to modernize and liberalize its economy and political system. It has spurred trade, investment, and overall economic integration between the United States and Mexico. And in a more modest way it has enhanced American productivity and prosperity—refuting the critics who were wrong 10 years ago and who are just as wrong today.

NO: The trade deficit caused by NAFTA has slowed the economy, resulting in the loss of hundreds of thousands of U.S. jobs.
By William R. Hawkins

In the days following the terrorist attacks of Sept. 11, 2001, security at U.S. borders was increased. American factories across the country suddenly were contemplating shutting down because the flow of parts and components from plants in Mexico was slowing to a trickle. Without the production capacity that had shifted to Mexico following passage of the North American Free Trade Agreement (NAFTA), large blocks of the U.S. manufacturing sector were paralyzed. Luckily, corporate protests to the White House put cross-border trade back on a more "business-as-usual" basis.

Most of the debate about NAFTA has focused on the direct loss of American jobs as Mexican laborers earning less than $2 an hour replace American workers making five or six times as much, plus health and pension benefits. Though there are specific trade disputes with Canada, the United States' NAFTA partnership to the north does not receive the same kind of fundamental criticism. Income and living conditions are similar in Canada, which puts trade on a more level playing field.

Every week new evidence of problems with Mexico is reported in local newspapers across the United States. For example, it wasn't a very merry Christmas for the 1,177 employees who were laid off from the LG. Philips Displays plant in Ottawa, Ohio, just before the holidays. Nancy Morman, who had worked at the plant for 32 years, lost more than her paycheck. She will lose two-thirds of her retirement package because at age 50 she is too young to qualify for full retirement. This is a reminder that it is not just lower wages in Mexico but the desire to avoid paying pension benefits that make a movement south of the border attractive to parsimonious firms.

> *Every week new evidence of problems with Mexico is reported in local newspapers across the United States.*

Is this really what economists mean when they talk of comparative advantage as a good thing? In theory, comparative advantage has a country concentrating its resources in those sectors in which it is most productive, then trading some of the output for imports of goods that other countries are better at producing. Trade with underdeveloped countries, however, often is determined by low-cost production stemming from conditions that generally are considered to be negative, such as a desperate and impoverished workforce, corrupt officials, and lax regulations governing everything from worker safety to environmental quality.

The great success of America has been the elevation of the industrial "working class" into middle-income status. It is a triumph that has given the United States an unprecedented record of social and political stability as well as economic pre-eminence. But it is being challenged by a globalization process that sees America's success as a point of commercial vulnerability to be attacked.

The aggregate impact of hundreds of cases such as that of LG. Philips Displays is measured by the trade deficit with Mexico, which has exploded since NAFTA was implemented. In 1993, the United States ran a small $1.8 billion trade surplus with Mexico. That the U.S. trade surplus with its southern neighbor had been falling in recent years was used by NAFTA proponents to argue that reducing Mexico's trade barriers would put the U.S. surplus back on an upward course.

One of the most famous predictions was made by Gary Hufbauer of the Institute for International Economics, a well-financed "free-trade" think tank. Hufbauer claimed that "NAFTA will generate a $7 billion to $9 billion surplus that would ensure the net creation of 170,000 jobs in the U.S. economy the first year." This did not happen, of course, and as the *Wall Street Journal* reported in its Oct. 26, 1995, edition, "Gary Hufbauer . . . whose predictions of NAFTA job gains were embraced by the Clinton and Bush White Houses, now figures the surging trade deficit with Mexico has cost the U.S. 225,000 jobs."

One should not really talk about jobs in such a context, but job opportunities. Under normal circumstances, subject to the vagaries of the business cycle and to external shocks, a developed economy such as that of the United States will tend toward full employment. That means the U.S. economy creates around 2 million jobs a year, as people have to work at something to make a living.

It is foreign firms and overseas workers who increasingly are supplying U.S. demands in the most productive and lucrative industries.

The adjustment mechanism is the wage rate. At what wage level will the labor market clear? One would think that given the almost magical progress made in technology in recent decades, and the cooling of inflation, real wages would be on the rise. Alas, this has not been the case.

According to the 2002–2003 edition of *The State of Working America* by Lawrence Mishel, Jared Bernstein, and Heather Boushey, real wages in 2001 were lower than they had been in 1979. This is due to two main factors: the change in the composition of the workforce as high-paying manufacturing employment fell as a share of labor relative to lower-paying services, and the chilling effect on wage increases in domestic manufacturing due to foreign competition.

On the surface, American manufacturing seems to be thriving. From 1987 to 2000, productivity for the manufacturing sector rose nearly 60 percent—but output rose only by about 40 percent, indicating that the sector overall was shrinking. The motor-vehicle and parts industry boosted its productivity by 37 or 44 percent between 1987 and 2000, depending on whether productivity is measured on a per-worker or per-hour basis. But again, output increased by less than the productivity gain as foreign imports of cars and parts increased, a process in which Mexico played a role.

Americans still have a hunger for manufactured goods. The country is becoming service-oriented only in employment, not consumption. Unfortunately, it is foreign firms and overseas workers who increasingly are supplying U.S. demands in the most productive and lucrative industries. As my colleague at the U.S. Business and Industry Council, Alan Tonelson, has shown, from 1997 to 2000 virtually no American industries gained domestic market share from foreign competitors despite their impressive gains in productivity.

In 2000, the United States imported more than $1 trillion worth of manufactured goods, including $196 billion in cars and auto parts, and $347 billion in capital goods and equipment. The result was a $452 billion trade deficit in goods, the measure of the net loss to the United States in industrial capacity and job opportunities. The trade numbers only have gotten worse since, and the U.S. goods deficit easily will surpass $500 billion for 2002.

Federal Reserve Board Chairman Alan Greenspan has called the trade deficit "unsustainable." Both the International Monetary Fund and the 17-nation Organization for Economic Cooperation and Development warned this fall that the U.S. trade deficit poses a danger to the stability of the world economy because of the financial strain it puts on the dollar. The usual "market solution" to such an imbalance is a currency collapse and a deep recession.

Every month the Federal Reserve Bank of St. Louis reports the extent to which the trade sector has slowed the American economy. Those who cite only exports as a pro-growth factor are misleading the public in the same way a sportscaster would be if he reported only the number of points scored by the home team. A football team might feel proud of scoring 27 points, but if the opposing team scores 43, it's still a loser.

According to the 2002 *Economic Report of the President*, "In 2000 net exports depressed real GDP [gross domestic product] by 0.8 percentage points." The domestic economy was strong enough in 2000 to overcome the negative impact of the trade deficit and still grow, but it would have done better if trade had been balanced, and perhaps avoided the recession.

The $24.6 billion U.S. trade deficit with Mexico in 2000 was not the main cause of the overall deficit, but it was a contributing factor and a complete refutation of the prediction that NAFTA would improve the United States' international accounts. In 2000, the U.S. automotive trade deficit with Mexico was $24 billion. General Motors, Ford, DaimlerChrysler, Delphi Automotive Systems, and other leading automakers and parts suppliers (including many non-American) have major operations in Mexico. Other major manufactured exports from Mexico include electronic products and telecommunications equipment.

The Clinton administration made a fundamental mistake in thinking that Mexico was a "big emerging market" that required only reforms to open it to U.S. exports. It confused population with purchasing power. Mexico is a low-income country, burdened by debt and suffering a trade deficit of its own that limits its ability to increase imports for domestic consumption without risking another in a series of financial crises. In such a situation, the only practical way for an American company to sell to Mexican consumers is from factories built inside Mexico. The customers with the most money, however, are the corporations that have set up maquiladoras. Exports to them measure not the expansion of U.S. industry, but its dispersion across the border.

Mexico's trade deficit with the rest of the world indicates another failure of NAFTA. A strong argument made during the NAFTA debate was that American firms needed a low-wage export platform in Mexico to combat Asian rivals—mainly Japan—that were expanding production in Southeast Asia.

But Mexico has remained an export platform directed only at the United States, not at markets in Asia or Europe. Instead, Asian and European firms have set up their own maquiladora plants, the better to flood the American market. This is the primary reason Mexico runs a trade deficit. It imports parts and equipment from Japan, South Korea, and Germany but does not send exports back to those countries. Instead, the foreign goods are used to produce exports shipped to the United States. In 2000, Mexico sent 91 percent of its exports to the United States, compared with 3 percent to Europe and only 1 percent to Asia.

The American political elite has invested so heavily in NAFTA with Mexico that it cannot admit the deal produced none of the predicted improvements in the U.S. position. Instead, it actually added to the trade problems the country has been experiencing for more than a decade.

Now there is a drive to escalate integration with Mexico, erasing the border as much as possible. Washington feels it must bail out Mexico's financial system but dares not enforce its own immigration laws, lest it cast doubt on the wisdom of this southern strategy. Thus every aspect of U.S. relations with Mexico will continue to deteriorate and impose increasing costs on the American people.

Economists See NAFTA As Being Beneficial for U.S. Jobs

By Christopher Swann
Financial Times, February 24, 2004

The case against the North American Free Trade Agreement is simple to make and easy to understand. Perhaps for that reason, it seems to be a favourite of some U.S. politicians on the stump—most recently, John Edwards, the North Carolina senator and presidential hopeful, who has made the claim that U.S. jobs have been lost because of NAFTA a central theme of his campaign.

However, many economists see things differently. While jobs have been lost in some sectors, they say the agreement's overall impact has been beneficial. As Gary Hufbauer, a senior fellow at the Institute for International Economics think-tank in Washington, points out: "The problem for advocates of the pact is that the losers from free trade are easy to identify and have faces, whereas those who have benefited are invisible and unaware they have been helped. The costs are highly concentrated and the gains are larger but diverse."

Because the benefits of free trade are delivered by countries focusing on areas in which they have a comparative advantage, some gross job losses from free trade are inevitable. If workers are able to move smoothly from declining to growing sectors, however, this should be more than offset by net job creation elsewhere.

"Since the U.S. is widely seen as the world's great example of a flexible labour market, it might be expected to be a beneficiary from free trade," says Bruce Kasman, head of economic research at JP Morgan.

Between 1993 and 2003, trade within NAFTA doubled, while trade by NAFTA countries with the rest of the world has risen by 42 per cent. If some Americans have seen their jobs disappear it is because they have been undercut on price, says Mr Hufbauer.

"This means cheaper goods, which raises the spending power of everyone else and this should be positive for employment," he says. "It makes no sense for the U.S. to be producing goods that can be produced elsewhere more cheaply."

Many economists say some U.S. manufacturers would have shifted parts of their production to lower cost countries even without NAFTA.

Privileged access to the Mexican market has increased the efficiency of some U.S. companies, particularly the car sector, says Sidney Weintraub, of the Center for Strategic and International Studies. "The U.S. auto industry has gained significantly from a better division of labour and advantages of scale," he says.

For those who have lost their jobs, the economic arguments are cold comfort. A study in 2001 suggested that many displaced workers were forced to accept lower paid jobs. About 36 per cent found jobs that matched or surpassed their previous salary but 25 per cent suffered wage losses of 30 per cent.

"The lower skilled have felt the pointy end of competition," says Mr. Kasman.

Estimates of the job losses vary. One recent study suggested NAFTA might have displaced about 110,000 workers every year. Mr. Hufbauer thinks this is an exaggeration.

An aid programme set up for U.S. workers adversely affected by trade and investment with Canada and Mexico—the Transitional Adjustment Assistance Program—has been claimed by about 50,000 a year. This is a relatively small number in an economy with about 130 million workers. Even in 1999, when unemployment was at a 30-year low, a total of 2.5 million U.S. workers lost their jobs.

Instead of renouncing free trade, economists say there should be more assistance to retrain workers who need to change sectors.

Mr. Weintraub says that adjustment, rather than trade itself, should be the focus for policy.

"One reason protectionism has been so close to the surface in the U.S. is that there is so little assistance for people who are displaced," he says.

Mexico: Was NAFTA Worth It?

By Geri Smith and Cristina Lindblad
BusinessWeek, December 22, 2003

Piedad Urquiza probably doesn't know much about NAFTA, but she knows what it's like to have a steady job. Urquiza works at a Delphi Corp. auto-parts plant in Ciudad Juárez, just across the border from El Paso. The assembly line is a cross section of working-class Mexico, from twentysomethings raised in this border boomtown to veteran hands harking from the deep interior. In the years since NAFTA lowered trade and investment barriers, Delphi has significantly expanded its presence in the country. Today it employs 70,000 Mexicans, who every day receive up to 70 million U.S.–made components to assemble into parts. The wages are not princely by U.S. standards—an assembly line worker with two years' experience earns about $1.90 an hour. But that's triple Mexico's minimum wage, and Delphi jobs are among the most coveted in Juárez. "I like the environment, I like my colleagues," says Urquiza, a 56-year-old widow who assembles the switches that control turn signals. The daughter of a poor rancher, she dropped out of school after the seventh grade and has relied on her Delphi job to raise six children to adulthood—and, she hopes, to a better life.

Urquiza and millions of other Mexicans live out daily one of the most radical free trade experiments in history. The North American Free Trade Agreement ranks on a par with Europe's creation of the euro and China's casting off Marxism for capitalism. It encompasses 421 million people and melds two first-world economies—the U.S. and Canada—with a struggling third-world country, Mexico. The bloc was seen as a bold attempt to demonstrate once and for all free trade's vast power to turn a developing nation into a modern economy. If anything was a litmus test for globalization, NAFTA was it.

Promises, Promises

On Jan. 1, NAFTA will celebrate its 10th anniversary. The assessment? The grand experiment worked in spades on many levels. American manufacturers, desperate for relief from Asian competition, flocked to Mexico to take advantage of wages that were a 10th of those in the U.S. Foreign investment flooded in, rising to an annual average of $12 billion a year over the past decade, three times what India takes in. Exports grew threefold, from $52 billion to $161 billion today. Mexico's per capita income rose 24 percent, to just over $4,000—which is roughly 10 times China's. "NAFTA gave us a big push," Mexican president Vicente Fox told *Business Week*. Fox notes proudly that Mexico's $594 billion economy is now the ninth-largest in the world, up from No. 15 a dozen years ago. "It gave us jobs. It gave us knowledge, experience, technological transfer."

Just as important, the pact spurred profound political change. Mexicans who backed open markets also wanted an open political system. Would the Institutional Revolutionary Party (PRI) have fallen from seven decades in power in 2000 if Mexico hadn't signed a treaty requiring government transparency, equal treatment for domestic and foreign investors, and international mediation of labor, environmental, and other disputes? It's hard to believe democracy would have come as quickly without NAFTA.

Impressive milestones—and seemingly ample proof that free trade delivers the goods. But rightly or wrongly, a large proportion of Mexicans today believe the sacrifices exceeded the benefits. The Mexican mood is infecting other Latin countries, which after 15 years of gradually opening their own economies to trade and investment are showing pronounced fatigue with the "Washington consensus," the free-market formula preached by the U.S. and the International Monetary Fund. In an August poll of 17 Latin countries carried out by Chile-based Latinobarómetro, just 16 percent of respondents said they were satisfied with the way market economics were working in their countries. Thus NAFTA's perceived shortfalls are giving fresh ammunition to free trade's opponents. "Now you have a whole network of people organizing against the Free Trade Area of the Americas and globalization because of what has happened in Mexico under NAFTA," says Thea Lee, the AFL-CIO's chief expert on international trade pacts. That's an ironic switch: It was NAFTA, after all, that kicked the free trade movement into high gear, spurring forward the Uruguay round of global trade talks in the mid-1990s and setting the stage for China's entry into the World Trade Organization in 2001.

Why have so many Mexicans soured on NAFTA? One problem is that the deal was oversold by its sponsors as a near-magic way to turn Mexico into the next Korea or Taiwan. Ten years later, many

Mexico: Then & Now	
Despite doubts among Mexicans, the benefits under NAFTA are numerous	
1993	**2003**
GOVERNMENT	
Single-party dominated	Multiparty democracy
GROSS DOMESTIC PRODUCT	
$403 billion	$594 billion
EXPORTS AS % OF GDP	
15%	30%
OIL AS % OF EXPORTS	
18%	9%
REMITTANCES BY MIGRANTS IN U.S.	
$2.4 billion	$14 billion
Data: Mexican Central Bank, Economist Intelligence Unit	

think the pact has stopped paying dividends—and that Mexico has been unfairly neglected by a Washington consumed by the war on terror. Speaking before an audience of Mexican students on Nov. 11, Mexico's envoy to the U.N., Adolfo Aguilar Zinser, characterized NAFTA as "a weekend fling." The U.S., he said, "isn't interested in a relationship of equals with Mexico, but rather in a relationship of convenience and subordination." While Zinser's remarks cost him his job, his words struck a chord. In an October survey by a leading pollster, only 45 percent of Mexicans said NAFTA had benefited their economy. That's down from the 68 percent who in November 1993, saw the pact as a strong plus. With the U.S. in a slump for the past three years, Mexicans are experiencing the downside of their close commercial ties with the colossus. Mexico's economy will grow by 1.5 percent this year, a poor showing for a developing country.

> *Only 45 percent of Mexicans said NAFTA had benefited their economy.*

Mexicans are feeling aggrieved because they see themselves simultaneously ignored by American policymakers while being yoked more firmly to the U.S. economy than ever. With the U.S. in a slump for the past three years, that has been a hard relationship to endure. Mexico's economy will grow by 1.5 percent at best this year, a poor showing for a developing country.

In a larger sense, Mexicans feel shortchanged by globalization. They thought they would be America's biggest workshop. That honor now belongs to China, which this year surpassed Mexico as the U.S.'s No. 2 supplier. Mexican policymakers signed trade agreements with a total of 32 countries, and as a result consumers got cheaper and better goods. Yet local manufacturers of everything from toys to shoes, as well as farmers of rice and corn, struggle to survive the onslaught of cheap imports. Mexicans hoped NAFTA would generate enough jobs to keep them at home. Instead, the jobless flock in ever-greater numbers across the border. Reforms that pressed on Mexico before NAFTA—modernizing the electricity sector, overhauling the tax code, shoring up the crumbling schools—are an even more difficult sell now that power is split among several parties.

Opportunity Knocked

Do Mexico's woes disprove the value of free trade? Few would argue that NAFTA was a waste. "If we didn't have NAFTA, we'd be in far worse shape than we are today," says Andrés Rozental, president of the Mexican Council on Foreign Relations. If NAFTA has disappointed, it is in part because the Mexican government has failed to capitalize on the opportunities it offered. "Trade doesn't educate people. It doesn't provide immunizations or health care," says Carla A. Hills, the chief U.S. negotiator in the NAFTA talks. "What it does is generate wealth so government can allocate the gains to things that are necessary." If a government doesn't allocate new wealth correctly, the advantages of free trade quickly erode. That is Mexico's plight. "NAFTA wasn't an end unto itself but a means to something, and that something was precisely the need to go further in reform," says former Mexican president Carlos Salinas, one of NAFTA's principal architects. "It's like Alice in Wonderland—you have to run faster and faster if you want to stay in the same place. Globalization won't wait for you."

The outcome of Mexico's struggle to regain momentum is of vital interest not just to Latin America but also to the U.S. The Bush administration has made trade a key part of its hemispheric agenda. Besides, the U.S. needs a stable, prosperous Mexico on its border to stem the flood of illegal immigration and drugs. Mexico's ability to get to the next stage will also show whether low-wage economies around the globe can hold their own against China. "Mexico cannot compete sewing brassieres and tennis shoes," says Roger Noriega, U.S. Under Secretary of State for the Western Hemisphere. "They cannot compete with China—who can? Mexico has to modernize so it can move forward."

NAFTA has already proven a powerful impetus to reform. Mexico did not hike its import tariffs when the peso crisis of 1994 hit. Encouraged, Washington stepped in with a $40 billion bailout package that helped Mexico stabilize its finances and return to the capital markets in just seven months. Although wrenching, the devaluation turbocharged NAFTA by dramatically lowering the costs of Mexican labor and exports. The government's fiscal discipline has earned the country a coveted investment-grade rating on its debt. And the current recession is mild by historic standards. Most analysts see growth quickening to 3.5 percent next year.

Yet even with a rebounding economy, Mexico will not generate enough jobs to accommodate its fast-growing workforce. While U.S. companies praise the work of their Mexican employees, they now make it abundantly clear that there are other, cheaper locales. An assembly worker in Mexico

The Great Migration

Mexican immigrants residing illegally in the U.S.

1990: 2.04 million
2000: 4.81 million

Data: U.S. Citizenship & Immigration Services

earns $1.47 an hour; his counterpart in China makes 59 cents an hour, according to a new report by McKinsey & Co. Top Delphi executives have warned for months that some work may be shifted to China because of the many advantages it offers. "Delphi and other automotive suppliers are courted every day by other countries, not only with lower-cost labor but also with new incentives and tax breaks," says David B. Wohleen, president for Electrical, Electronics, Safety & Interior. "Mexico will need to significantly pick up the pace to remain a competitive alternative," he warns.

No one feels the China threat more keenly than Daniel Romero, president of the National Council of the *Maquiladora* Export Industry. Mexico's *maquiladoras*, which assemble goods for export using imported parts and components, have been around since the mid-1960s. Under NAFTA, the number of plants rose 67 percent, to 3,655 in just seven years. Yet more than 850 have shut down since 2000 with many shifting to cheaper locales. Employment is down more than 20 percent from its peak of 1.3 million workers. Romero and a group of *maquiladora* managers traveled to China last year, and came away dispirited. "They have aggressive tax incentives, low salaries, very aggressive worker training, and a supply chain that allows them immediate access to the latest technology," says Romero.,

The agriculture sector is suffering even more than the *maquiladoras* as subsidized U.S. food imports flood the country. Some 1.3 million farm jobs have disappeared since 1993, according to a new

---

"Society at large and a good chunk of the economy have failed or refused to adjust to globalization."—Luis Rubio, head of a Mexico think tank

---

report by the Carnegie Endowment for International Peace, a Washington think tank. "NAFTA has been a disaster for us," says Julián Aguilera, a pig farmer from Sonora. He and his peers have staged big demonstrations to protest a 726 percent increase in U.S. pork imports since the pact took effect. "Mexico was never prepared for this."

Nor was the U.S. As the *campesinos* lost their livelihood, they headed to the border. By most estimates, the number of Mexicans working illegally in the U.S. more than doubled, to 4.8 million between 1990 and 2000. Despite tightened security after September 11, hundreds of thousands of Mexicans continue to cross the border. The money sent back to their families will hit $14 billion this year, more than the $10 billion Mexico expects in foreign direct investment.

The exodus has turned rural hamlets into ghost towns. Panindícuaro in Michoacán, one of Mexico's poorest states, has one of the highest incidences of migration with one out of every seven people leaving. Panindícuaro's priest, Melesio Farías, recently said mass for a young father who died trying to cross the Arizona desert. "I tell them to forget the U.S. and to work at home," says Farías. "But if Mexico can't offer them jobs, why should they?"

Salinas' band of technocrats and their successors didn't do enough to prepare vulnerable sectors for NAFTA's onslaught. Long-promised programs to help 20 million *campesinos* switch to export crops never materialized. Nor has the government offered inducements to channel investment into areas where it is most needed. The six border states, along with the capital, nabbed 85 percent of foreign outlays last year. Little has been done to foster local suppliers for the import-dependent *maquiladoras*. Less than 3 percent of the industry's parts are sourced in Mexico. "Society at large and a good chunk of the economy have failed or refused to adjust to globalization," argues Luis Rubio, who heads the Center of Research for Development, a Mexico City think tank. "And the government has done absolutely nothing to help."

This laissez-faire attitude is in stark contrast to China. There, state-owned banks have bankrolled lavish investments in industrial parks, power plants, highways, and other infrastructure to provide low-cost facilities for foreign manufacturers. These multinationals had to source as many components as possible from domestic suppliers, and the government wasn't bashful about demanding transfers of technology to Chinese partners. As a condition for entry into the WTO in 2001, China is phasing out these policies, but domestic companies now have a headstart.

Even if China-style tactics are not possible, Mexico could still hone its competitiveness. The PRI under Salinas took advantage of its monopoly on power to ram through painful reforms that paved the way for NAFTA. Now under a multiparty system, the politicians struggle to make difficult choices. Mexico will need to spend $50 billion to upgrade its power grid. But legislation to open the constitutionally protected sector to private investment has run into nationalist sentiment and union opposition, even while electricity rates are as much as 40 percent higher than in China. Grupo México, the world's third-largest copper producer, is considering moving refining operations to Amarillo, Tex., where electricity costs 4 cents per kilowatt-hour versus 8.5 cents in Sonora.

Education is another critical area where reform has stalled. William Spurr, head of the North American transport division of Canada's Bombardier, which builds railcars in Hidalgo, sees a need for more skilled workers. "There's a very good talent pool, but there aren't enough of them," he says. "If I opened a plant in India, I'd have all the engineers and technicians I need."

To be fair, the government's finances have been sapped by a $100 billion bailout after the peso crisis. Even under those circumstances, the number of science and engineering college grads has nearly doubled over the past decade, to 73,300. Yet that number still pales next to

Report Card

Percentage of Mexican students finishing high school:

1993: 20%
2003: 28%

Data: Mexican Ministry of Education

India, which graduated 314,000 students in those subjects, while China handed out diplomas to 363,000. Congress has so far foiled Fox's efforts to raise taxes to improve education.

To get a glimpse of what the right training can do, consider the case of Tecnomec Agrícola, a maker of farm and earth-moving equipment based in Aguascalientes, in central Mexico. "We never had a tradition of exporting. NAFTA definitely changed that," says founder José Leoncio Valdés. It was hard going at first. "We couldn't get in to see people in the U.S. because we were from Mexico and they figured we were unreliable," recalls the 55-year-old engineer. Then in 2000, Valdés dispatched his son José to earn a degree in engineering and business administration at Massachusetts Institute of Technology. On his first spring break, young José conducted a weeklong session with two dozen Tecnomec managers. He used Lego blocks to build a replica of the factory and figure out how to better track inventory, boost quality, and control waste. Tecnomec soon boosted productivity by 21 percent. Now its exports total $1.4 million a year, nearly a quarter of annual sales.

Mexico could use more Tecnomecs. Just 50 companies account for half of all exports—and the top tier is dominated by multinationals. Thousands of other Mexican businesses have gone under in the face of competition. "We are at a watershed," says Jaime Serra Puche, Mexico's chief NAFTA negotiator. "Either we take the steps to become a true North American country or we just become a big Central American country."

Serra Puche is one of prominent Mexicans trying to figure out how to improve NAFTA. "If we were going to do it all over again today, I would insist on introducing a lot of considerations," says President Fox, who believes that NAFTA should be modeled more on the European Union, with provisions for free movement of labor and cross-border grants to compensate poorer countries for dislocations. Proposals for a single currency and a North American energy cooperation plan have also surfaced. But don't expect any breakthroughs soon—not while the U.S. heads into elections and trade has reemerged as a contentious issue.

So for now the burden will remain on Mexico. Salvador Kalifa, an independent economist based in Monterrey, recalls that when the conquistador Hernán Cortés reached Mexico, he burned his boats to prevent crew members from fleeing. "With NAFTA, we burned our boats and threw ourselves into globalization," says Kalifa. "There is no turning back."

What Happened When Two Countries Liberalized Trade? Pain, Then Gain

By Virginia Postrel
The New York Times, January 27, 2005

Economists argue for free trade. They have two centuries of theory and experience to back them up. And they have recent empirical studies of how the liberalization of trade has increased productivity in less-developed countries like Chile and India. Lowering trade barriers, they maintain, not only cuts costs for consumers but aids economic growth and makes the general public better off.

Even so, free trade is a tough sell. "The truth of the matter is that we have one heck of a time explaining these benefits to the larger public, a public gripped by free trade fatigue," the economist Daniel Trefler wrote in an article last fall in *The American Economic Review*.

One problem, he argued, is that there is not enough research on how free trade affects industrialized countries like the United States and Canada. Another is that research tends to concentrate on either long-term benefits or on short-term costs, instead of looking at both.

"We talk a lot about the benefits of free trade agreements, but when it comes to academics studying it, we know next to nothing in terms of hard-core facts about what happens when two rich countries liberalize trade," Professor Trefler, of the Rotman School of Management at the University of Toronto, said in an interview.

His article, "The Long and Short of the Canada–U.S. Free Trade Agreement," uses detailed data on both Canadian industries and individual companies to address these gaps. (The paper is on his Web site at *http://www.economics.utoronto.ca/trefler/*.) The study looks at the effect of tariff reductions, the simplest kind of liberalization.

Tariffs are usually not considered that significant in developed countries, where many major industries compete without such protection. But, Professor Trefler said, "they're not significant except where they matter."

Before the agreement went into effect in 1989, more than one in four Canadian industries were, in fact, protected by tariffs of more than 10 percent. Those industries included not only businesses known for their protectionism, notably apparel makers, but manufacturers of a wide range of products, from beer and pretzels to coffins, plastic pipes, and paper bags.

Before the agreement, imports from the United States faced an average tariff of 8.1 percent and an effective tariff of 16 percent. The effective rate included import taxes on the final product and tariffs paid on raw materials. Someone importing a chair could face a direct tariff on furniture, for example, but could also pay indirect tariffs on wood and upholstery fabric.

Not surprisingly, the Canadian industries that had relied on tariffs to protect them "were hammered" when those barriers disappeared, Professor Trefler said. "They saw their employment fall by 12 percent," he said, meaning one in eight workers lost their jobs. In manufacturing as a whole, the trade agreement reduced employment by 5 percent.

"Employment losses of 5 percent translate into 100,000 lost jobs and strike me as large," he wrote, "not least because only a relatively small number of industries experienced deep tariff concessions."

High-productivity Canadian manufacturers not only expanded into the United States but further improved their operations.

No wonder free trade agreements touch off so much opposition.

As painful as those layoffs were, however, the job losses were a short-term effect. Over the long run, employment in Canada did not drop, and manufacturing employment remains more robust than in other industrialized countries.

"Within 10 years, the lost employment was made up by employment gains in other parts of manufacturing," Professor Trefler found.

While low-productivity plants shut down, high-productivity Canadian manufacturers not only expanded into the United States but further improved their operations. Along the way, they hired enough new workers to make up for losses elsewhere.

"The average effect of the U.S. tariff cuts on Canadian employment was thus a wash: the employment losses by less-productive firms offset the employment gains by more productive firms," Professor Trefler wrote in an e-mail message, citing further research.

Nor, contrary to predictions, did Canadian wages drop because of competition from less-educated, nonunionized workers in the southern United States. Quite the opposite: using payroll statistics, he found that "for all workers, the tariff concessions raised annual earnings" by about 3 percent over eight years.

Admittedly, that is not a lot. "A 3 percent rise in earnings spread over eight years will buy you more than a cup of coffee, but not at Starbucks," he wrote. "The important finding is not that earnings went up, but that earnings did not go down." In addition, he said, "there is absolutely no evidence" that the trade agreement worsened income inequality.

The big story is that lowering tariffs set off a productivity boom.

Formerly sheltered Canadian companies began to compete with and compare themselves with more-efficient American businesses. Some went under, but others significantly improved operations.

The productivity gains were huge. In the formerly sheltered industries most affected by the tariff cuts, labor productivity jumped 15 percent, at least half from closing inefficient plants. "This translates into an enormous compound annual growth rate of 1.9 percent," he wrote.

But closing plants is not the whole story, or even half of it. Among export-oriented industries, which expanded after the agreement, data from individual plants show an increase in labor productivity of 14 percent. Manufacturing productivity as a whole jumped 6 percent.

"The idea that a simple government policy could raise productivity so dramatically is to me truly remarkable," Professor Trefler said.

And the long-run increase in productivity did not result mostly from shutting down inefficient plants. It came from better operating practices.

"That's not coming from natural selection," he said. "That firm's actually doing business differently."

Thanks in part to the trade agreement, he sees a shift in attitudes among the younger generation of Canadian managers. They are less content to be the best in Canada's relatively small market.

"They're thinking the competition isn't here in Toronto," he said. "The competition is there in the U.S. To succeed in U.S. markets, you have to play like the Americans do, which is innovate and upgrade."

III. FTAs with Latin America

Editor's Introduction

Though a unified consensus has yet to emerge concerning the wisdom of NAFTA and free trade in general, the United States government, like its counterparts in other nations, has remained committed to forging additional FTAs. As negotiations within the World Trade Organization (WTO) for a global FTA have stalled, the U.S. has moved toward smaller bilateral agreements, targeting the nations of Latin America in particular. But the United States is not the only country with such designs on Latin America; with its vast supply of cheap labor, the region is seen as a valuable potential resource by other industrialized nations. Chapter 3 discusses some of the more controversial FTAs being established in Latin America—not only by the U.S., but also by the European Union (EU).

As the U.S. seeks to establish other FTAs around the world and agrees to open its markets to foreign countries, it must attempt to safeguard its interests. Intellectual property rights, environmental protection, and corporate stewardship are all important issues that the U.S. government considers when negotiating trade agreements. Stumbling blocks emerge, however, when potential partner countries perceive that acceding to American demands could adversely impact their own interests.

The first article in this chapter, "U.S. Officials Focusing on Smaller Free Trade Agreements," discusses the various matters negotiators consider when entering into FTAs. As talks continue over the Free Trade Area of the Americas (FTAA) and the Central American Free Trade Agreement (CAFTA), U.S. representatives try to ensure that they do not sacrifice the nation's interests in the name of free trade.

Although once a priority, FTAA talks have stalled over the past year due to the divergent needs of the various countries involved. Some participants blame the U.S. for the lack of progress, citing the American government's refusal to curtail its agricultural subsidies; in turn, U.S. representatives attribute the impasse to the unwillingness of certain countries to open their service sectors to foreign competition. The second piece in this section, "Hemispheric Trade Zone Stumbles," examines these issues, as well as the United States' decision to pursue smaller trade agreements while the FTAA talks are stalled. In the subsequent entry, "Offshoring Closer to Home," Roger Morton examines the proposed Central American Free Trade Agreement, which would lower trade barriers between the United States and the nations of Costa Rica, Honduras, El Salvador, Nicaragua, Guatemala, and the Dominican Republic. While CAFTA has yet to be approved by Congress, Morton believes that the reelection of President George W. Bush augurs well for its eventual passage.

The EU has also sought FTAs in Latin America, and one of them is covered in the next article, "EU-Mercosur Trade Deal Crashes on the Rock of Tariffs," which examines the problems that have developed during negotiations for an initiative that would remove trade barriers between the EU and the nations of Brazil, Paraguay, Uruguay, and Argentina. This agreement has floundered due to the unwillingness of the Latin American countries to open their service sectors and because of conditions recently proposed by EU negotiators regarding import quota expansion. The final entry in this chapter, "Still Taking Root," examines MEUFTA, an agreement between Mexico and the EU which went into effect on July 1, 2000. Presently seen as an opportunity wasted, this four-year-old agreement has yielded few tangible results and has been overshadowed by the potential EU-Mercosur FTA.

U.S. Officials Focusing on Smaller Free Trade Agreements

By Brian Stempeck
Greenwire, December 4, 2003

Although U.S. officials hope to finish a major Central American free trade pact next week, trade experts say most work next year will be on smaller bilateral agreements between the United States and foreign nations, as progress has slowed on World Trade Organization and Free Trade Area of the Americas (FTAA) negotiations.

"Unfortunately, we seem to be somewhat stalled in the WTO right now," said a GOP aide to the Senate Finance Committee earlier this week at a trade roundtable. "There does not seem to have been a lot of progress made since Cancun."

"The WTO needs to be nudged along," added a Democratic aide to the House Ways and Means Committee. The collapse of WTO talks in September shows a need for a "more incremental approach" to global trade negotiating, the aide said.

WTO negotiations in Cancun, Mexico, broke down in September, as poor and rich nations failed to reach a compromise on farm subsidies. Ministers from the 146 countries left five days of negotiations without advancing the global trade accord that began in Doha, Qatar, in November 2001. The negotiations included WTO proposals to reduce or eliminate tariff and non-tariff barriers to environmental goods and services, such as catalytic converters, air filters, and consulting services for wastewater management (*Greenwire*, Sept. 15).

Similarly, congressional aides said recent meetings in Miami dealing with FTAA—which would lower tariffs and other trade barriers between 34 countries in North and South America—demonstrated that those talks have also lost momentum. FTAA participants initially hoped to conclude negotiations, which began in 1994, by 2005, but that deadline now appears unlikely. The Senate aide called FTAA "a very ambitious undertaking."

Some South American countries, including Brazil, want an FTAA agreement that addresses only tariffs, whereas the United States seeks a broader agreement dealing with investment rules, intellectual property, and other issues. Also, Brazil is seeking an FTAA agreement on agricultural subsidies, which U.S. representatives feel would be better handled by the WTO (*Greenwire*, Nov. 17).

With slow progress on WTO and FTAA, the staffers said Congress will likely consider two or three free trade agreements next year, dealing with Morocco, Central America, and potentially Australia. Congress affirmed FTAs with Chile and Singapore this year. "We are now focused almost exclusively on relatively small bilateral agreements," the House aide said.

The White House is close to the finish line with one broader trade agreement, however. U.S. trade officials hope to complete the Central American Free Trade Agreement (CAFTA), aimed at reducing trade barriers between the United States and Costa Rica, El Salvador, Honduras, Nicaragua, and Guatemala, by the end of the year. A final round of meetings with Central American officials begins Monday.

Environmental regulations have become a factor in CAFTA negotiations, as Senate Democrats, led by Sen. Max Baucus (D-Mont.), have lobbied the administration to include stronger environmental regulations in CAFTA than the regulations found in the Chile and Singapore FTAs.

> *"We are now focused almost exclusively on relatively small bilateral agreements."*—an
> **aide to the House Ways and Means Committee**

In late November, Baucus and 20 other senators sent a letter to U.S. Trade Representative Robert Zoellick calling on the Bush administration to include environmental protections in CAFTA to make it more similar to the North American Free Trade Agreement (NAFTA). Baucus and other senators feel that CAFTA should include public participation requirements similar to those in NAFTA, which give individuals and nongovernmental organizations the ability to call for an investigation if a government is not enforcing environmental laws.

Lawmakers would also like to see stiffer corporate stewardship requirements, requiring companies to provide information about the discharge of toxic chemicals, for example, and forcing companies to publicize the amount of money they paid for the right to mine natural resources.

Another major trade issue is an obscure investment provision included in NAFTA, and likely to be in CAFTA, which allows foreign companies to challenge rules or regulations they feel unfairly limit their ability to do business. The so-called Chapter 11 investment provision allows these challenges to be heard by three-member international tribunals that meet behind closed doors, which environmentalists have assailed as giving corporations the power to dodge environmental laws.

When Congress approved "fast track" trade negotiating authority last year, it required that new trade agreements provide for "an appellate body or similar mechanism" in the investor-state dispute resolution process, and lawmakers want the administration to create that appellate body in the CAFTA agreement.

The Senate GOP aide said that Senate Finance Committee Chairman Chuck Grassley (R-Iowa) is still weighing Baucus' suggestions. "There are some suggestions worth looking at," the aide said. "I think there are reasonable solutions."

But the aide also predicted that other issues—especially opposition from U.S. textile manufacturers and sugar producers—could play a larger role in determining whether Congress affirms CAFTA next year.

The House aide agreed that other issues will likely play a larger role than the environment, but said the creation of an appellate body for the international tribunal is an imperative. The administration has said it wants to work the appellate process into the context of a larger trade agreement, such as FTAA, but some House members feel the issue should be addressed sooner than that, the aide said. Currently, international tribunals could issue conflicting decisions, as there is no high court—such as the Supreme Court in the United States—to resolve differences.

The final round of CAFTA negotiations begins Monday in Washington, D.C.

Hemispheric Trade Zone Stumbles

By Danna Harman
The Christian Science Monitor, November 23, 2004

President Bush returned to the U.S. after a long weekend of talks in Latin America Monday, having addressed, at least briefly, several long-neglected regional issues: Mexican immigration, the war on drugs, and China's increasing influence on the continent. But one subject he skirted was the plan for a Free Trade Area of the Americas (FTAA), once a chief ambition of his administration.

President Clinton launched negotiations in 1994 for the creation of a 34-country hemispheric single market stretching from Alaska to Argentina, intended to be operational by 2005. The Republicans, even more ardent enthusiasts of free trade than their Democratic predecessors, had said, before Sept. 11, 2001, that the plan was a priority.

The hope was that the FTAA would function like an extended NAFTA (the North American Free Trade Agreement between the U.S., Mexico, and Canada) or CAFTA (the not-yet-ratified Central American version between the U.S., Guatemala, Honduras, El Salvador, Nicaragua, Costa Rica, and the Dominican Republic). But it turns out not all were buying.

The initiative has stalled, as much because of the 9/11 hijackers and the war in Iraq as the diverging economic ideologies of North and South America. As U.S. politics has drifted to the right in recent years, the South has, in large swaths, leaned left—in turn favoring smaller, bilateral treaties.

Last week, Eduardo Duhalde, President of Mercosur—a trade bloc of Brazil, Argentina, Uruguay, and Paraguay—blamed the standstill on Washington's unwillingness to stop giving generous subsidies to U.S. farmers. He was responding to strong words from U.S. trade representative Robert Zoellick, who said Mercosur has refused to open up such service sectors as banking, telecommunications, and transport.

Mr. Zoellick further warned that Mercosur risked being isolated as the U.S. clinched one-on-one and regional free trade agreements with a host of other Latin American countries. Indeed, the U.S. and others are increasingly focusing time and effort on narrower pacts around the world. "When we came into office, we had free trade agreements with three countries—Canada, Mexico, and Israel,"

Zoellick said this weekend. "We now have concluded free trade agreements with 12 countries and we are negotiating with 12 more. So, we're busy on that front."

In Latin America, besides NAFTA and CAFTA, the U.S. has also signed a bilateral agreement with Chile; is in negotiations with Peru, Colombia, and Ecuador; and is hoping to start talks with Bolivia.

The trade agreement with Chile is often cited by the U.S. as a model. Under it, 85 percent of qualifying consumer and industrial goods passing between the two countries are now duty free, with the remaining tariffs to be phased out over the next 12 years. This year, U.S. exports to Chile were up some 25 percent, and Chile's exports to the U.S. were up 27 percent. Chile's $72 billion economy grew 3.3 percent last year, and this coming year it could hit 5.5 percent.

Chile, clearly warming to the model, has struck similar deals with the European Union and South Korea, has others in the works with New Zealand and Turkey, and announced just last week that it would start talks with China.

Beyond the tactics of how to open markets both fairly and evenly, the arguments over the benefits of free trade continue.

But whether such smaller agreements can serve as precursors to a broader hemispheric agreement, or if they actually hurt those chances, is under debate. Some observers urge caution when looking to these pacts as harbingers for successful broader accords.

"Yes, [the U.S.–Chile accord] seems to be working— but let's wait two or three years to say anything definite," says Peter Hakim, president of the Inter-American Dialogue in Washington. "After 10 years of NAFTA and a host of reputable studies, debates are still furious about whether and how much the accord benefited Mexico," he continues, noting that rising commodity prices this year—especially copper—may have had a lot to do with the growth of the Chilean economy.

Stuart Harbinson of the World Trade Organization is pessimistic about the smaller deals. "This expanding web of [regional trading arrangements] raises the question of workability of parallel multilateral approaches," Mr. Harbinson told reporters, adding that there are today 150 regional trade agreements in force and another 70 in the works, all of which vary widely, despite efforts to adopt "best practices." Such a multitude of pacts tends to raise production costs because businesses have to comply with a variety of rules. The WTO, with strong U.S. backing, is pushing to sign all countries up for the Doha round—the latest phase of trade liberalization conducted on a global level.

Beyond the tactics of how to open markets both fairly and evenly, the arguments over the benefits of free trade continue. In downtown Santiago, just blocks from malls full of Starbucks and TGI Friday's, the streets were crowded over the weekend with thousands of antiglobalization protesters railing against the destruction of local jobs and culture by the corporate forces driving the free trade agenda.

And just outside of the Chilean capital, the national sport was being played in cheerful defiance of the creep of a homogenized global culture. At the Puro Caballo rodeo, men in colored ponchos and wide-brimmed hats competed in a sport that dates back to the early 19th century. The idea is for two-man horseback teams to maneuver a bull around the ring and slam it against the padded side.

Alberto Romero has just placed second in the first round and is sitting on a haystack, pointing out the nuances of the sport to his 11-year-old son. During the week, this cowboy is the buttoned-up CEO of a company that sells luggage and baseball caps. He has a concession from Austria, imports the cloth from Asia, manufactures in Chile, exports to Argentina, and is currently evaluating entry into the U.S. market.

He is pleased with the bilateral agreements Chile has and makes use of them. "I'm a global businessman," he says, flinging a short white jacket around his shoulders. "Would a FTAA make life easier?" Probably, he says, but just thinking of getting those negotiations done "gives me the kind of headache I bet that rodeo bull has right now."

Offshoring Closer to Home

By ROGER MORTON
LOGISTICS TODAY, JANUARY 2005

As the new Congress convenes this month, it is anticipated there will be a quick (for a governmental body) passage of the Central American Free Trade Agreement (CAFTA) and signing by the White House. The agreement is similar to the North American Free Trade Agreement (NAFTA) but took just one year of negotiation, while the U.S.–Canada–Mexico pact took seven years of talks.

CAFTA members are Costa Rica, El Salvador, Guatemala, Honduras, Nicaragua, and joining at the last minute, the Dominican Republic. The last-named is a curious addition to the treaty, since the other five countries are joined at their borders on the American isthmus, while the Dominican Republic—part of the Caribbean Basin Trade Preference Act—shares its landmass with Haiti on a Caribbean island. However, the Dominican Republic has the largest economy in the Caribbean and, combined with Haiti, a vigorous textile industry.

"The role of the governments in Central America will be to take advantage of CAFTA to accelerate the industrial evolutionary process," explains Dan Gardner, president Latin America, freight management division for third-party logistics provider (3PL) Exel (*www.exel.com*). "Costa Rica is a prime example, with [chipmaker] Intel Corp. coming into the country several years ago. The country has been able to build upon that in terms of Intel attracting its supplier base to Costa Rica around that primary manufacturing entity."

As with other suppliers of integrated services, Exel conducts business in the CAFTA region on two levels. First, it enables international commerce, both inbound and outbound. Second, once material and product is within the region, it offers transportation and domestic infrastructure for warehousing and distribution.

"We're optimistic about Central America because it has a unique geographic location relative to the U.S.," notes Charlie Dominguez, vice president for sales and marketing for Latin America with Crowley Maritime Corp. (*www.crowley.com*). "It has a common language in all of its countries. We also expect a lot of growth between the countries. We expect them to be cost effective in terms of this hemisphere. When you can deliver a garment in five or six days, door-to-door, that's very competitive, with only the border operations of Canada and Mexico being faster."

CAFTA is a two-way trade agreement, Dominguez points out, offering U.S. manufacturers and retailers the opportunity to sell their goods into those six countries.

For now, the trade agreement will be focused largely on textile and apparel operations for the CAFTA countries, particularly since the World Trade Organization is lifting restrictions on Chinese apparel exports beginning this month. Under intense pressure from Washington and other countries, the Chinese government announced at the end of 2004 that it would levy export taxes on some of its manufactured textiles, giving the rest of the world a reprieve, for the moment.

It's believed that CAFTA nations will enjoy a distinct geographic advantage over Asian apparel producers. All CAFTA countries have enjoyed peace for more than a decade and have worked to improve infrastructure and attract more business.

"Over the past two or three years, Nicaragua has had an incredible growth—over 30 percent annually in the maquilla sector alone," points out Bernardo Callejas, senior investment advisor for manu-

---

CAFTA nations will enjoy a distinct geographic advantage over Asian apparel producers.

---

facturing operations for ProNicaragua (*www.pronicaragua.org*), a governmental agency. "In 1998, we had approximately 18,000 workers in maquillas. Today, we have more than 65,000 workers."

Suppliers of products complementary to the apparel industry are moving into Central America so that manufacturers don't have to shop for services and supplies—instead, they're integrated into the countries.

Interestingly, as Callejas notes, particularly for jean manufacturers, Mexico is outsourcing some apparel work to CAFTA members. "Mexican businesses look to Central America, their little brother, where they can make the same garment for a lot less expense than in Mexico," he observes.

Exel's Gardner is optimistic about long-term possibilities of CAFTA. "Geographic proximity to markets is a huge advantage," he says. "Central America is a maximum of a three-hour flight or two-day sailing from the U.S. In terms of lead-time management and the importance of lead-time as part of replenishment programs for any type of industry, this is extremely important."

EU-Mercosur Trade Deal Crashes on the Rocks of Tariffs

By Mario de Queiroz
IPS—Inter Press Service, October 21, 2004

It took just an eight-hour meeting in the Portuguese capital and a 25-line communique to destroy the last remaining vestiges of hope, after five years of efforts, of reaching a free trade agreement between the European Union and South America's Mercosur trade bloc before the current members of the European Commission step down.

The new EU Commission headed by former Portuguese prime minister Jose Manuel Durao Barroso (2002–2004), which takes office Nov. 1, will continue the complex negotiations on a date to be set in the first quarter of 2005, after a technical-level meeting before the end of this year.

The basic concept underlying the meeting "was the effort to explore the limits of the negotiations, something that had not been sounded out before," added the minister.

According to Mercosur representatives, the EU has set new conditions for expanding its quotas of imports of some farm products, while the EU sees the South American bloc's proposal for opening up the automobile industry, service sector, and government procurements as overly limited.

On the agricultural trade front, the touchiest area in the talks, the powerful European lobbies, led by the intransigent French position, have raised the main obstacles to an agreement.

In formal diplomatic language, the brief statement issued at the end of the meeting at around midnight Wednesday said substantial progress had been made, but "there is still much to do before reaching the required level which the strategic importance of this accord between the EU and Mercosur reflects."

Taking part in the meeting in Lisbon were European commissioners for trade and farming, Pascal Lamy and Franz Fischler, foreign ministers Celso Amorim of Brazil and Leila Rashid of Paraguay, deputy foreign minister William Ehlers of Uruguay, and Argentina's Secretary of Trade and International Economic Relations Alfredo Chiaradia.

Speaking with the press after the meeting in the wee hours of Thursday morning, Lamy and Amorim alluded to the description by analysts of Oct. 20 as "the last chance" to sign an agreement.

The negotiations were about substance, not deadlines or timetables, and they will continue to be pursued by our successors, just as we inherited them from our predecessors, said Lamy, referring to the upcoming replacement of the European Commission, the EU executive arm.

> *Economists on both sides of the Atlantic say a free trade deal would be an important boost to trade.*

Brazilian Minister Amorim, speaking in the name of his counterparts from Argentina, Paraguay, and Uruguay—the other full members of Mercosur (Southern Common Market)—put special emphasis on "the strong political will, and the significant progress" made in Lisbon.

Both sides "showed great flexibility on some points, which was not sufficient to reach an accord, but was sufficient to allow us to be optimistic, because the strong interest in reaching an agreement, shared by both blocs, was made clear," said Amorim.

He also underlined that "Mercosur spoke with one voice," independently of specific national interests in each of the bloc's member countries.

The talks have dragged on for five years without any concrete results.

Economists on both sides of the Atlantic say a free trade deal would be an important boost to trade between the two blocs, which currently exceeds $40 billion a year.

If an accord is reached next year, the world's biggest free trade area would be created, with nearly 700 million people.

But in a recent interview with the *Diario Economico*, a Lisbon newspaper, Brazil's ambassador to the World Trade Organisation (WTO), Jose Alfredo Graa Lima, said it would be preferable for Mercosur to wait for the multilateral trade talks in the WTO to advance before agreeing to an accord with the EU.

Portuguese economic analyst Alfredo Valladao said, "The diplomats on both sides are convinced of the need for this agreement, but have been unable to confront the clamour from those who do not want any accord."

"The negotiators of the (EU) Commission want to close the deal because they believe that a Mercosur based on an EU-style blueprint could be the ideal ally for promoting a more multilateral world," he added in an analysis published Wednesday.

But the EU is also aware that guarantees are necessary for exports and investment in Mercosur "due to the dangers posed by a future Free Trade Area of the Americas (FTAA), because without such guarantees it would be like handing over control to the United States," warned Valladao.

Negotiations for the FTAA, which would comprise all countries of the Americas with the exception of Cuba, have virtually come to a standstill.

Lamy and Amorim presented an upbeat image at the end of Wednesday's meeting, saying "areas of possible flexibility" were explored.

According to Lamy, the meeting's big achievement was the strong level of confidence and trust that was reached. "The question today is very simple: do we stop the train or do we carry on?" he added, underlining that both sides chose the second alternative.

Still Taking Root

By Matthew Brayman
Business Mexico, August 2004

Last month, Mexico's deal with the largest economic bloc in the world passed an anniversary, but instead of champagne celebrations and giddy profit counting, insiders lamented four years of missed opportunities.

Hailed as a trade coup at its inception on July 1, 2000, the Mexico-EU Free Trade Agreement (MEUFTA) has since gone widely forgotten, according to finance leaders and diplomats on both sides of the Atlantic. And the European Union's deal with Mercosur (on schedule to be in place within 18 months) threatens to transform Mexico from a vanguard in Euro–Latin American relations to an outsider.

"I think (MEUFTA) has been a very underutilized and underpublicized agreement for reasons that escape me," Andres Rozental, who has served as Mexican ambassador to Great Britain and Sweden and currently runs an international consulting firm, told *Business Mexico* in a telephone interview. "The EU and Mexican government authorities have not done a lot of work or taken advantage of the opportunities it offers, specifically in science, technology, and other cutting-edge business sectors."

Statistics support Rozental, as commerce between Mexico and the EU has not grown in the four years since the deal was signed. Over 80 percent of Mexico's imports and exports continue to circulate in the Americas, and any gains made in the European market have been largely the result of private-sector moxie rather than a sea change in how the two markets interact.

"I arrived here at the beginning of the trade agreement, and unfortunately trade has not grown," Elena Espinosa de los Reyes, a Bancomext representative and Mexico's commercial counselor to the United Kingdom for the past four years, told *Business Mexico* in an interview here [London]. "It grew a little at the very beginning, but then it just stabilized and in some cases even decreased. Certainly companies have not taken full advantage of the agreement."

It wasn't supposed to be this way. For Europe, the deal offered an opportunity to achieve some free trade parity with the United States, which enjoyed the inside track of NAFTA in addition to its geographical foothold. For Mexico and the political leaders who inked the accord, the deal was intended to propel Mexico into the enviable position of a center of commerce between the United States, Latin America, and Europe.

But this golden bridge connecting Mexico to the European Union, the largest integrated economy in the world that accounts for nearly one-quarter of global production, remains incomplete. Commerce between Europe and Mexico has never surged—for reasons of logistical difficulty, ignorance on the part of Europe as to what Mexico has to offer besides Cancun and handcrafts, and the excesses of Mexico's own deal-signing orgy. Although it leads the world with 43 free trade deals, these have been called nothing more than a gloss over deep economic problems by some observers.

"The problem for Mexico is that the signing of free trade accords has served as a substitute for development," the European Parliament stated earlier this year in a paper entitled, "Lessons Learned by the Trade Accord between Mexico and the European Union."

Failure to reform the energy sector, in particular, has discouraged investment, while nationalistic rants by Mexican lawmakers, in which outside criticism is often interpreted as an intrusion on the nation's sovereignty, have displeased many Europeans. "The EU is not a priority for the Fox government," the European Parliament said in its study, explicitly stating that MEUFTA had not lived up to expectations.

The World Bank also continues to criticize Mexico for low education levels, bad government, corruption, inadequate regulatory standards, poor infrastructure, and technological short-comings.

This negative perception of Mexico has mixed with logistical problems that inherently cripple transatlantic commerce, making any advances between the two markets laden with risk.

An Ocean Apart

Logistics invariably tops businesspeople's lists as the No. 1 enemy of increased Mexico-EU trade. Shipping time across the Atlantic takes at least 17 days, handicapping agricultural producers and other suppliers of perishable goods.

Exports to EU Countries (in millions of U.S. dollars)

Country	1999	2000	2001	2002	2003	Total '99-'03	Jan.-March 2004
Total EU	5,202.70	5,610.10	5,332.60	5,214.50	5,591.70	26,951.60	1,416.70
Germany	2,093.10	1,543.90	1,504.10	1,263.30	1,753.00	8,130.40	450.70
Spain	822.40	1,519.80	1,253.90	1,431.00	1,464.40	6,491.50	385.50
Belgium	240.70	227.00	317.80	295.80	137.30	1,218.60	37.00
Denmark	49.10	44.70	44.40	37.80	38.90	214.90	9.60
Austria	10.80	17.00	19.60	15.40	10.20	73.00	3.30

Source: Economy Secretariat

"If you are exporting to the United States, you just put it in a crate on a truck and maybe it takes 12 hours to get across the border. But with Europe, we are talking about transporting to the other side of the world," said Espinosa.

The proximity of Mexico to the United States and of European countries to one another fundamentally discourages Mexican and European exporters from getting involved in the Atlantic shipping lanes, choosing instead to stay in their own neighborhood. "In order to do business consistently, there is no alternative than to set up your own factory in the region," said Rozental.

An emboldened few Mexican companies have tackled this logistical problem by aggressively investing in Europe.

Tortillas in England and Mexican cement in Spain attest to their proficiency.

The Cemex Example

The shining example of that strategy is Cemex, widely considered a model of Mexican efficiency to the world and an illustration that conceptions of Mexico as backward and unsophisticated are unfounded.

Cemex, one of the top three cement companies in the world with operations in over 30 countries and trade relations with over 60 nations, is currently the leading cement company in Spain. It entered the market in 1992, acquiring Valenciana and Sanson, which were then Spain's two largest cement companies. These aggressive, transatlantic moves even predated the Mexican company's expansion into neighboring markets in Central and South America. At first intended simply to counter a European rival's expansion into the Mexican market, Cemex's Spanish incursion has blossomed into the cornerstone of the company's worldwide operations, with its 85 Spanish factories ranking second only to its Mexican operations and out-numbering its U.S. presence by 20 plants.

This astute recognition of the Spanish market, with its mountainous terrain and high transportation costs, has paid dividends for Cemex. Shipping bags of cement across the Atlantic was not a viable option.

Imports from EU Countries (in millions of U.S. dollars)

Country	1999	2000	2001	2002	2003	Total '99-'03	Jan.-March 2004
Total EU	12,742.80	14,775.10	16.165.50	16,441.60	17.861.90	82,499.60	4,512.70
Germany	5,032.10	5,758.40	6,079.60	6,065.80	6,274.90	30,890.20	1,679.40
Spain	1,321.80	1,430.00	1,827.40	2,223.90	2,288.30	9,663.20	571.80
Belgium	305.20	465.60	630.50	556.90	573.00	2,645.40	114.20
Austria	170.00	176.80	219.60	186.60	254.80	1,083.90	76.00
Denmark	126.50	142.00	169.20	177.40	198.80	864.40	50.50

Source: Economy Secretariat

In addition to the fruitful Cemex sojourn into Europe, the food-maker Maseca has set up operations in Coventry, England, from where it distributes tortillas throughout Europe, and the auto parts dealer Alfa has established profitable operations in Central Europe.

> *For political leaders, MEUFTA has been painted as a triumph*

But these companies are the exception rather than the rule, and for Mexico there still remain many opportunities as yet untapped in Europe, regardless of what politicians may tell the business community.

Don't Believe the Spin

For political leaders, MEUFTA has been painted as a triumph, and Foreign Relations Secretary Ernesto Derbez earlier this year said, "The accord has contributed significantly to our integration into the world economy and our dynamic export performance."

Mexico is indeed the seventh-largest exporter in the world, but the lack of creative business ties between Mexico and its European partners was glaringly obvious at the late May summit in Guadalajara between Latin American and European leaders. While Spanish Prime Minister Jose Luis Zapatero was remarking how an EU-Mercosur trade pact sits "on the launching pad" (expected to go into effect in January 2006), the only major reference to Mexico-EU commercial cooperation was a modest proposal presented by President Fox to help small- and medium-sized enterprises. The program, known by its Spanish acronym PIAPyMES, will have a budget of 24 million euros and will help small Mexican businesses get involved in Europe and vice versa. MEUFTA got nary a mention, as multinational-minded businessmen waxed realistic about what the once-considered trade deal has become.

"It really has turned out to be more of an investment facilitation agreement than anything else," said Rozental, who heads a consulting firm that specializes in multinational corporate enterprises in Latin America. (Rozental is scheduled to address AMCHAM members in a Face-to-Face in mid-August.)

Rozental was among the observers who said the May summit did little more than offer Mexico the opportunity to get to meet the 10 new EU members joining the 15 original members who signed the 2000 trade deal.

Something to Build On

The fact that there was a MEUFTA deal signed at all—and it did mark the first agreement between the EU and an American nation—testifies to Mexico's emergence as a major player on the international stage. But what it does to build on that early advantage will go a long way to determining its place in the global market.

Foreign Direct Investment in Mexico by Country and Economic Region
(in millions of U.S. dollars)

Country/ Region	1999	2000	2001	2002	2003	Jan.-March 2004
North America	7,715.80	12,584.30	21,504.40	8,608.60	5,516.40	1,587.80
Canada	623.30	664.70	988.10	184.90	161.80	-4.60
United States	7,092.50	11,919.60	20,516.30	8,423.70	5,354.60	1,592.40
European Union	**3,722.70**	**2,827.60**	**4,034.30**	**3,836.70**	**3,541.20**	**4,694.50**
Holland	1,008.50	2,582.80	2,558.20	1,153.30	465.80	20.60
Spain	997.20	1,909.50	754.20	407.70	1,389.20	4,546.20
Germany	753.10	344.40	-151.00	597.30	274.30	78.20
United Kingdom	-193.40	265.80	87.20	1,149.20	855.00	3.30
France	169.50	-2,520.90	386.90	170.20	315.60	0.00
Denmark	179.60	201.00	231.80	156.00	75.40	42.60
Other Countries						
Switzerland	124.60	132.90	130.20	422.00	315.50	1,073.90
Japan	1,232.60	416.80	178.30	149.70	97.70	5.10
Total FDI	**13,205.50**	**16,585.70**	**26,775.70**	**13,628.20**	**9,738.50**	**7,424.80**

Source: Economy Secretariat

"That comprehensive accord, which is beginning to demonstrate its potential, was possible in large part due to the unprecedented process of political reform and institutional renewal that Mexico went through in the past decade," Mexico's Ambassador to the United Kingdom Juan Jose Bremer—who has served as ambassador to five European nations over the past two decades—told *Business Mexico* in an exclusive interview.

"Although the presence of Mexico in the UK is growing, and the bilateral relationship is at a good level in the political, economic, and cultural areas, its real potential is not yet thoroughly exploited." Bremer said.

All in the Neighborhood

Progress on the EU-Mercosur deal—which several heads of state in the Americas and Europe have described as a priority—illustrates how Mexico, which at the turn of the millennium was considered LatAm's face to Europe, has transgressed and now sits in a perilous position.

With Brazil and Chile increasing their commerce with Europe and the Mercosur-EU deal getting closer to realization, Mexico must take advantage of this window of unrivaled trade opportunity to profit outside of the American hemisphere. Mexico has always been tied to its northern neighbor, and many insiders say that monolithic U.S. presence has deterred

European investors and led Mexican exporters—many of whom have factories just a stone's throw from the U.S. border—to balk at getting more involved in the European market.

"In Mexico, there is an enchantment with the United States, and Fox is down in Brazil (in mid-July) negotiating with Mercosur partners. Our immediate neighborhood is what has been important," said Rozental. "But Mexico is primarily a European-orientated country in terms of language, culture, and religion. Certainly its roots are there.

"However, on the European side, there has been the perception that Mexico is not worth making an effort for because Mexico has thrown its lot in with the United States. And that is very tough to compete with," he said.

A hint of European arrogance has also colored dealings with Mexico, whether it be decrees by the European Parliament that Mexico is "technologically weak" or statements from leaders that imply that Mexico must come to Europe, rather than the reverse. "Europe is an inevitable dimension to any sensible business plan." EU Ambassador to Mexico Nigel Evans said recently.

Positives in the Deal

Europe's private sector, however, has made moves to get involved in Mexico. In banking, Spanish BBVA took control of Bancomer earlier this year, while in the construction sector, the Swiss cement company Holcim took a page out of Cemex's book and purchased the Mexican firm Apasco.

And statisticians are quick to point out that numbers can be misleading. Europe has invested more in Mexico than the spreadsheets would imply, as investment is often made in Mexico through U.S. subsidiaries of European-based enterprises. Likewise, exports to and from Europe often pass through the United States in transit and are recorded as a U.S. import or export.

Regardless, there remains a lot to do in improving commerce, and even staunch supporters of Mexico-EU trade recognize that there is a ceiling on how far commerce can go between the two entities. "Because of time zone differences and exchange rate issues, I don't think the Europeans look at this as a market to conquer but rather as a platform (to the LatAm region as a whole)," said Rozental.

Although bilateral observers recognize the pitfalls and limitations of Mexico's relationship with the EU, there remains the sense that any gains made between the two sides—given Mexico's profitable relationship with the United States and its other neighbors—will serve as gravy for a country dependent on its exports.

"When you are talking about the largest trading bloc in the world, why shouldn't we be more involved in it?" said Bancomex's Espinosa. "It is not a matter of dividing our export cake differently, but rather a question of making it larger."

IV. FTAs Around the World

Editor's Introduction

Just as Latin America is not the only region of the world where free trade agreements (FTAs) are cropping up, the United States. and the European Union are not the only major powers pursuing such accords. Today, countless nations have bought into the idea of free trade and are actively seeking FTAs in the hopes of bettering their economic positions. Of these nations, China, with its vast reserves of inexpensive labor and emerging consumer culture, is blossoming into a major force in global economics and has become one of the most proactive countries in terms of forging FTAs, inking several prominent deals with its Asian neighbors. Other nations and regions, however, are just waking up to the current global fascination with FTAs; the Arab world, for instance, is beginning to seek out such accords. Chapter 4 discusses these issues, focusing on the emergence of FTAs throughout the globe, particularly in Asia and the Pacific Rim, as well as the emergence of new agreements in Islamic nations.

As the United States actively solicits FTAs all over the world, one region it has begun to set its sights on is the greater Middle East. A key battleground in the U.S. war on terror, many Middle Eastern countries currently receive a great deal of U.S. aid but little attention in the way of trade agreements. Many argue that FTAs between the United States and the Middle East would help U.S. allies in their relations with Muslim nations in ways that direct aid could not. Though initially reluctant, the United States is now committing itself to erecting trade agreements with more moderate Muslim countries in the region to promote democratic reform and economic opportunities. The opening piece in this chapter, "U.S. Eyes Free Trade Treaties in Gulf," looks at the issues surrounding the formation of FTAs between the U.S. and the Arab world.

Unlike their counterparts in the Middle East, the nations of eastern Asia are having no difficulty finding willing FTA partners. China in particular has actively sought FTAs throughout the continent, most recently entering into an agreement with 10 countries collectively known as the Association of Southeast Asian Nations (ASEAN). "New Trade Pact Could Cut Clout of U.S. in Asia" discusses this historic agreement, as well as how it may affect U.S. influence in the region in the future.

Just hours after China and the ASEAN nations agreed to their pact, Australia, Japan, New Zealand, and South Korea announced their intention to begin trade talks with ASEAN. In Chapter 4's next entry, Ian Mader discusses ASEAN's newfound prominence in global free trade, as well as the significance of ASEAN actively pursuing agreements with "economies that are siphoning foreign investment from the region."

Another important FTA being considered throughout Asia and the Pacific involves members of the Asia-Pacific Economic Cooperation (APEC). This 21-member group agreed to open trade by 2020, but this goal has stalled in favor of smaller, bilateral FTAs. The final article in this chapter, "APEC Members Differ over Route to Free Trade," examines the decision by some APEC members to focus on these smaller trade agreements, the problems this poses for APEC as a whole, and how APEC can begin to concentrate on global initiatives again.

U.S. Eyes Free Trade Treaties in Gulf

By Jeffrey Sparshott
The Washington Times, November 16, 2004

The Bush administration yesterday said it would negotiate free trade pacts with two Arabian Peninsula nations, taking steps toward a broader Middle East Free Trade Area.

The United Arab Emirates and Oman are politically moderate, oil-rich nations in an often troubled region.

"A free trade agreement with the UAE and Oman will promote the president's initiative to advance economic reforms and openness in the Middle East and the Persian Gulf, moving us closer to the creation of a Middle East Free Trade Area," U.S. Trade Representative Robert B. Zoellick wrote in a letter notifying congressional leaders of pending talks.

President Bush in May 2003 outlined a 10-year plan to create a U.S.–Middle East Free Trade Area to help promote democratic reform and expand economic opportunity in the region.

The United States already has a long-standing free trade agreement with Israel, the Clinton administration signed a free trade pact with Jordan in 2001, and the Bush administration has signed deals with Morocco and Bahrain.

The UAE is the United States' third-biggest trade partner in the Middle East, after Israel and Saudi Arabia, though the region in general is economically isolated.

In 2003 Oman was the 79th-biggest export market for the United States, and the UAE was 28th. Major U.S. exports include machinery, aircraft, vehicles, and electrical machinery, according to the U.S. Trade Representative. "These agreements are one part trade policy and 10 parts foreign policy," said Dan Griswold, director of the Cato Institute's Center for Trade Policy Studies, a Washington think tank that favors free trade.

"Outside of oil, we do relatively little trade with these countries, but the importance is symbolic. This is reaching out to moderate Arab states," Mr. Griswold said of Oman and the UAE.

Oman is a sultanate of 2.3 million people. The UAE is a federation of seven emirates with a population of about 4 million. The countries border Saudi Arabia and are across the Persian and Oman gulfs from Iran.

Mr. Zoellick yesterday notified Congress of the new negotiations, a necessary step before formal talks can begin. Under Trade Promotion Authority, the administration negotiates the agreements and submits them to Congress for a yes-or-no vote—no changes are allowed.

Trade pacts with the region enjoy bipartisan support among legislators. The Morocco deal, for example, passed the House 323–99 and the Senate 85–13.

In addition to creating some economic opportunity for U.S. firms, Mr. Zoellick said the agreements also would complement recommendations from the 9/11 commission's report. The report said the United States should expand trade with the Middle East to "encourage development, more open societies, and opportunities for people to improve the lives of their families."

Mr. Zoellick's office said formal negotiations are likely to begin next year.

New Trade Pact Could Cut Clout of U.S. in Asia

By Evelyn Iritani
Los Angeles Times, November 30, 2004

China inked a deal with 10 Southeast Asian countries Monday to create the world's largest free trade area, bolstering its influence in a region long dominated by the United States.

The leaders attending the Assn. of Southeast Asian Nations [ASEAN] meeting in Laos also announced plans to hold the first-ever East Asian Summit next year in Malaysia. The Asia-only gathering would include China, Japan, and South Korea.

The moves are likely to boost China's political and economic interests in an area where its relations have been strained by territorial disputes and lingering war animosities.

That could reduce U.S. clout among Southeast Asian nations that are key military allies and large markets for U.S. farm goods, machinery, and Hollywood films.

"This is a wake-up call," said Myron Brilliant, senior vice president of Asia policy for the U.S. Chamber of Commerce. "China is becoming more aggressive in its outreach to its neighbors, and we don't want to be left behind."

The free trade pact would lead to the elimination of tariffs by China and ASEAN on thousands of products by 2015.

China's "charm offensive"—which includes the development of bilateral trade pacts, increased investment in energy and raw materials producers, and expanded tourism and educational exchanges—has strengthened its standing as a regional leader at a time when U.S. policymakers have been distracted by the war in Iraq and terrorism, analysts said.

"By any aggregate measure, the United States is still the great power of Asia," said Kurt Campbell, senior vice president at the Center for Strategic & International Studies in Washington. "But if you go behind the scene in boardrooms, military councils, and diplomatic settings, you find that China's might and influence has grown almost exponentially in the last several years."

That change was evident during this month's meeting of the Asia Pacific Economic Cooperation forum in Santiago, Chile. Efforts by Asian business leaders there to push the concept of an Asia-wide free trade zone took a back seat to U.S. concerns over North Korea and Iran.

Nicholas Lardy, a China expert at the Institute for International Economics, said the Bush administration missed a valuable opportunity to use the APEC forum to counter the move toward an Asian-only trade bloc.

"Are we going to have a trade arrangement that draws a line down the middle of the Pacific or are we going to have a trade arrangement that includes the U.S.?" he said. "To the extent we don't use APEC to promote regional economic integration, by default we're going to have trade liberalization happening primarily within Asia."

The renewed interest in East Asian regionalism has been triggered by China's dramatic economic growth, which has led to a sharp increase in two-way trade with its neighbors. After the 1997 Asian financial crisis, sales of raw materials and components to China helped get its neighbors back on track.

> *The renewed interest in East Asian regionalism has been triggered by China's dramatic economic growth.*

At the same time, China has worked aggressively to increase its diplomatic profile in Asia, offering itself as a middleman in the North Korea nuclear dispute and seeking to defuse territorial disputes in the South China Sea.

With the U.S. preoccupied elsewhere, officials in Beijing have become more involved in setting the regional agenda, from the removal of trade barriers to establishing currency policies.

Li Fan, director of the World and China Institute, a non-government think tank based in Beijing, said the trade pact allows China to boost regional political stability and maintain good neighborly relations.

"North America and the European Union have their economic areas," he said. "Asia should have one."

ASEAN officials moved quickly Monday to quash concerns that the group was reviving a controversial plan by former Malaysian leader Mahathir Mohamad for an Asian-only economic group that would challenge U.S. dominance.

At a news conference, ASEAN Secretary General Ong Keng Yong told reporters the East Asian Summit was still at the "brainstorming" stage.

Charles Morrison, president of the East-West Center in Honolulu, described the summit's creation as a "natural evolution" in Asia's development that didn't necessarily threaten U.S. involvement in the region.

"This would be of concern to the United States if it looked as if Asia was uniting against the United States, but this one doesn't have that flavor," he said.

Under the trade pact, the six largest members of ASEAN—Singapore, Indonesia, Malaysia, Brunei, Thailand, and the Philippines—agreed to cut tariffs on 4,000 categories of goods to between zero and 5 percent by 2010. The four poorest countries—Laos, Vietnam, Cambodia, and Myanmar—have until 2015. Governments are given leeway to move more slowly in lowering tariffs on their most sensitive products, such as sugar, steel, and automobiles.

The implications for U.S. firms are not yet clear, business leaders said.

If the pact leads to increased economic growth, that could benefit U.S. farmers, high-technology companies, and others anxious to expand their sales to the region. U.S. multinationals with operations in China would also gain if they could export products to Southeast Asia with lower tariffs.

But if Chinese or Southeast Asian firms are given preferential treatment, particularly in heavily protected sectors such as agriculture or manufacturing, it could put U.S. competitors at a disadvantage, experts said.

Japan, South Korea, Australia, New Zealand Sign on for Free Trade Talks with ASEAN

By Ian Mader
Associated Press, November 30, 2004

Japan, Australia, and two other Pacific Rim economies joined the rush to court Southeast Asia, agreeing Tuesday to launch free trade talks with the region's leaders hours after they clinched a momentous market-opening deal with booming China.

The four nations—also including South Korea and New Zealand—signed accords with the 10-member Association of Southeast Asian Nations at their summit in Laos to launch talks early next year, aiming for trade pacts within two years.

Australian prime minister John Howard stressed that his country bore no ill will toward Southeast Asian nations despite his refusal to heed ASEAN's calls to join its nonaggression treaty, which he has dismissed as a relic of the Cold War.

"We have no hostile intentions towards anybody in the region," Howard said.

Some countries in Southeast Asia, especially Malaysia, have been wary of Howard because of his comments in 2002 that he reserves the right to launch pre-emptive attacks in countries if terrorists there threaten his citizens.

But the retirement last year of former Malaysian prime minister Mahathir Mohamad, who had often-icy relations with Howard, brought an improvement in Australia's ties with Kuala Lumpur, and its first ever invitation to an ASEAN summit.

Mahathir's successor Abdullah Ahmad Badawi said Australia will likely be invited again for next year's summit in Malaysia.

Tuesday's accords came a day after ASEAN and China signed a pact aimed at phasing in the world's largest free trade area by decade's end—a sprawling market of nearly 2 billion people.

The Southeast Asian group's secretary-general, Ong Keng Yong, said it would expand trade between the regions from about $100 billion this year to as much as $140 billion by 2010.

The agreement not only opens markets, but eases fears that China would be a "strategic bully" in the region, said Denny Roy of the Asia-Pacific Center for Security Studies in Hawaii.

"China has also tried to sell Southeast Asia on the idea that China's economic development is more of an opportunity than a threat to the region," Roy said. "The prevailing view seems to be that China is so far living up to its claim that it will not be a strategic bully as it grows more powerful."

The pact aims to bring tariffs below 5 percent in most of the 11 countries by 2010—giving an extra two years for prized products such as cars, and granting an extra five years for poorest ASEAN members Cambodia, Laos, Myanmar, and Vietnam to come on line.

Before closing the summit late Tuesday, ASEAN also adopted a blueprint for economic cooperation with India. Free trade talks with New Delhi began last year and are expected to take another year.

The agreements with China and India reflect desires by Southeast Asia to latch onto economies that are siphoning foreign investment from the region.

Communist Laos—holding its first-ever conference of this magnitude—eased its tight security on the final day of the summit in Vientiane, where dusty roads have been dotted with green-clad troops.

ASEAN members Brunei, Cambodia, Indonesia, Malaysia, Myanmar, Philippines, Singapore, Thailand, and Vietnam joined host Laos for the summit. Closed-door meetings opened Monday with an ASEAN-only session, followed by summits through Tuesday with partners China, Japan, South Korea, and India, Australia, and New Zealand.

APEC Members Differ over Route to Free Trade

By Heda Bayron
Voice of America News, November 16, 2004

Asia-Pacific leaders will face challenges posed by a wave of bilateral free trade agreements when they meet for their summit in Chile Saturday. The issue could threaten broader trade liberalization goals agreed to 10 years ago by the bloc of nations in the Asia-Pacific Economic Cooperation forum.

The Asia-Pacific Economic Cooperation forum, or APEC, set a goal 10 years ago in Bogor, Indonesia, to fully open trade by 2020.

Now a decade later, APEC's 21 member economies are a long way from that goal—following a global trend, which has stalled the World Trade Organization's efforts to open up trade.

Shujiro Urata, an economics professor at Waseda University in Japan, says slow progress has frustrated some countries into taking bilateral action.

"So many countries under APEC thought the way to liberalize was to go for a bilateral free trade agreement and other regional agreements," said Shujiro Urata.

The result is a proliferation of trade deals.

About half of APEC's members have signed at least one bilateral free trade agreement. Of 184 regional and bilateral agreements completed or negotiated worldwide in recent years, 79 involve APEC members. Proponents of the deals argue that they are building blocks toward wider free trade areas.

But some regional experts warn the deals undermine APEC's very foundation.

Professor Mark Beeson studies multilateral cooperation among Asia-Pacific nations at Queensland University in Australia.

"The fundamental premise that APEC was organized on, was some form of multilateral organization where various countries cooperated to achieve collective goals and the whole principle was based on non-discrimination," said Professor Beeson. "Bilateralism is the complete antithesis of that. It provides special benefits to two members of one deal and by implication excludes other people."

The challenge, experts say, is to ensure that bilateral and regional trade deals do not discriminate against other APEC members.

Chile, host of the annual APEC summit this year, is proposing a formal free trade agreement or a trade bloc among APEC members. This could create the world's largest trade zone, involving three of the biggest economies—Japan, China, and the United States.

Trade liberalization under APEC is currently voluntary.

Economist Fernando Gonzales-Vigil in Peru heads a task force studying regional trading for the independent policy group, Pacific Economic Cooperation Council. He says it is time for APEC to make bold decisions on freeing trade.

Trade liberalization under APEC is currently voluntary. Mr. Gonzales-Vigil says this limits what the group can achieve.

"When the agenda is so huge, when the agenda has very sensitive sectors, you are not able to go further up to a certain limit, voluntarily. If you want to go beyond a limit, you have to do it necessarily through binding negotiations done under the basis of reciprocity," he said.

Thus, some economists say, the bigger and more powerful WTO remains the primary platform for free trade because it enforces compliance.

Some are optimistic that the Bogor goals can be achieved, especially by developing economies. Developed nations may face more difficulties because of politically sensitive protected sectors such as agriculture.

So, how should APEC position itself in the debate over global versus bilateral deals? Professor Beeson at Queensland University says APEC's strength perhaps lies not in its trade role.

"I think APEC's great advantage is that it provides a forum in which all of the major players in the region can get together in one setting and can have important discussions," added Professor Beeson. "If APEC takes this role more seriously and perhaps doesn't worry about the trade agenda quite as much, then it could still be a potentially important organization."

APEC was formed in 1989 to advance cooperation among Asia-Pacific economies as fears grew that protectionism would increase as the old General Agreement on Tariffs and Trade was being phased out in favor of the WTO.

Leaders meet in Santiago, Chile, on November 20.

APEC comprises Australia, Brunei, Canada, Chile, Hong Kong, Indonesia, Japan, Malaysia, Mexico, New Zealand, Papua New Guinea, Peru, South Korea, the Philippines, Russia, Singapore, Taiwan, Thailand, the United States, and Vietnam.

V. The Broader Impact
of FTAs

Editor's Introduction

Though strictly economic in nature, FTAs have the capacity to impact a society on a variety of levels. Indeed the ramifications of these accords can fundamentally alter not just a nation's economy, but its political, environmental, and social structures as well—and not always for the better. This chapter looks at the effects FTAs can have on a society, especially developing countries, and how inconsistencies in policies between governments can prove disastrous when not remedied.

The United States has been exceedingly diligent in taking steps to protect the intellectual property (IP) rights of its citizens when negotiating FTAs. Clauses within such accords ensure that countries respect U.S. IP rights and refrain from the illegal use of copyrighted or patented material. The first two articles in this chapter debate the effects of U.S. IP protection on America's FTA partners. In the first article, "Why FTAs Are Bad for the Poor," Jakkrit Kuanpoth argues that developing countries should refrain from FTAs that impose these strict IP standards. Emphasizing the generic drug controversy that is at the heart of the debate between developing and industrialized countries, Kuanpoth states that FTAs "undermine the foundation of multilateral trade liberalization." Jim Mendenhall responds to Kuanpoth's arguments with "In Defence of FTAs," the second entry in this chapter. In contrast to Kuanpoth, Mendenhall believes that IP protection spurs innovation, attracts foreign investment, integrates developing countries into the global economy, and protects consumers from counterfeit products.

In addition to IP protection, the United States has also sought environmental safeguards when drawing up its FTAs. Despite the precautions taken by the United States, environmental degradation is sometimes an outgrowth of certain FTAs. The next four articles in this chapter specifically address the environmental impact of FTAs. The first piece, "The FTAA and the World," examines the debate surrounding the inclusion of environmental protection provisions in FTAs and the charge of "green protectionism" by developing countries that followed. The second article, "Why Are Some Trade Agreements 'Greener' than Others?" examines how two similar environmental incidents were handled by two distinct free trade bodies—NAFTA and the EU. The next article, "Paying for NAFTA," looks at how NAFTA has been detrimental to the Mexican environment. Many worry that the Mexican example is a harbinger of what is to come in other developing nations entering into similar FTAs. In "Truckers Worry About Equal Requirements," concerns about the standards—environmental and otherwise—of Mexican trucks entering the United States are discussed.

Along with environmental excesses, human rights abuses sometimes go hand in hand with FTAs involving developing countries. Stories of long hours, little pay, and termination for outspoken behavior abound. Though human rights abuses are illegal under most FTAs, enforcing those policies is difficult in politically unstable countries. The Mexican fear that U.S. companies will relocate to China in pursuit of cheaper labor is the topic of "Workers Say Rights Denied as Firms Threaten to Pull Out." This fear has, some say, spurred human rights abuses and sweatshop conditions. In response, the Mexican government has taken measures to improve conditions. The final article in this chapter analyzes the effects NAFTA has had on the poor, with a particular emphasis on how it impacts women, and what consequences the Free Trade Area of the Americas (FTAA) might be on women throughout the Western Hemisphere.

Why FTAs Are Bad for the Poor

By Jakkrit Kuanpoth
Managing Intellectual Property, June 2004

The neo-liberal orientation of free trade has reappeared in a new form as free trade agreements (FTAs). Why does the U.S.—the world's largest and strongest economy—want to have bilateral FTAs with small economies such as those of Singapore, Chile, Morocco, and Thailand?

One of the important things the U.S. is trying to achieve in its FTA negotiations is to establish an acceptable framework for trade that it cannot do within the WTO. The U.S. wants to create a new paradigm of IP protection, which is more stringent than the TRIPs [Agreement on Trade-related Aspects of Intellectual Property Rights] regime (the so-called TRIPs-plus standards).

TRIPs-plus expands the scope of IP protection. It ensures strict protection for biotechnology and pharmaceutical companies, copyright and trade mark owners, and authors and composers, but sets conditions for compulsory licensing that are more restrictive than under TRIPs and restricts parallel imports. This means that a country that signs an FTA with the U.S. will no longer be able to take advantage of the exemptions and options available under TRIPs. In particular they will no longer be able to interpret TRIPs provisions on access to essential medicines in a flexible way, a flexibility reaffirmed by the Doha Declaration on TRIPs and Public Health. At the same time, they will be prevented from taking safeguard measures against foreign rights holders, especially in such key sectors as pharmaceuticals and biotechnology.

Once a country signs an FTA with the U.S., it is required to protect plants, animals, biological processes and products, genes, and gene sequences. Countries that agree to patent biotechnological products and accede to UPOV [International Union for the Protection of New Varieties of Plants] Convention on plant variety protection may allow foreign interests to exert monopolistic power over these essential subjects and limit the country's ability to produce food crops. Since an FTA gives private companies the right to obtain monetary damages for government measures, any attempt by the government to regulate biotechnology products, such as issuing warnings about GM foods, could result in the government being sued by foreign investors under an investor-state dispute settlement system.

In the field of pharmaceuticals, many developing countries face difficulties in ensuring a stable supply of essential medicines. Signing an FTA will exacerbate the country's public health problems. This is because FTAs usually require extension of the patent term (particularly for pharmaceutical patents), restricting compulsory licensing and parallel imports, and exclusive protection for undisclosed test data. Data exclusivity would restrict companies from using test data previously submitted by multinationals to register generic versions of the same drug. This will undoubtedly delay the introduction of generic medicines into the market. The experiences of many poor countries led to adoption of the Doha Declaration. These experiences should make developing countries cautious about entering into such deals.

Bilateral trade deals are also being used to create new concepts of copyright protection. The FTA demands exclusive rights over work available online. Countries must provide effective remedies against people who circumvent technological measures used to guard works from unauthorized use. The copyright owners must have the right to take legal action against Internet service providers over copying of works by subscribers, and the right to track and trace digital copying. The worst change is the demand for rights against temporary reproduction, which could turn a range of activities—from temporary storage in electronic form, browsing or using the Internet—into copyright infringement.

FTAs are allowing copyright owners to extend control over access to works that have fallen into the public domain. The agreement also extends the conventional economic rights of the author to the right to use the work and distribute circumventing devices. This will greatly affect the public right of fair use with respect to digital works.

In view of the severe effects on the economy, society, culture, and educational development of the developing countries, and due to the lack of good governance and transparency in the FTA negotiation process, the WTO's member states must find a way to eliminate the trend towards FTAs, which in the long term may undermine the foundation of multilateral trade liberalization that each member advocates.

In Defence of FTAs

By Jim Mendenhall
Managing Intellectual Property, September 2004

Professor Jakkrit Kuanpoth's article "Why FTAs Are Bad for the Poor" [in June's *MIP*] grossly distorts the facts about IP standards included in U.S. free trade agreements (FTAs).

Jakkrit ignores the potential of IP protection to spur innovation and the development of indigenous industries, attract foreign investment, integrate developing countries into the global economy, and protect consumers from defective counterfeit products. India's software and film industries would be far less competitive were it not for India's strong copyright laws. When Jordan, a recent FTA partner with the U.S., adopted data exclusivity protection—one area that Jakkrit singles out for criticism—innovative medicines were brought to market faster than they ever were before. Intellectual property rules can thus be an engine of growth and raise standards of living.

Jakkrit seems to believe that FTA rules were pulled from thin air. In fact, most grew out of about a dozen existing international IP agreements. He attacks rules requiring protection of plant varieties, failing to note that the TRIPs Agreement [Agreement on Trade-related Aspects of Intellectual Property Rights] requires such protection and that UPOV [International Union for the Protection of New Varieties of Plants] is the system most commonly relied upon outside patents. He claims that FTAs "create new concepts of copyright protection," but fails to note that these concepts are derived from, for example, principles codified decades ago in the Berne Convention, and from two other treaties negotiated in the mid-1990s in the World Intellectual Property Organization.

Turning to the specifics of Jakkrit's critique, he claims that IP rules undermine a country's ability to deal with public health problems, by, for example, limiting grounds for issuing compulsory licences or restricting parallel imports. However, FTAs with Australia and Singapore permit the issuance of compulsory licences to address national health emergencies as well as for purposes of public non-commercial use. Recent U.S. FTAs with developing countries—Chile, Morocco, Bahrain, and Central America—do not contain any restrictions on compulsory licensing. Nor do the FTAs with these developing countries, with the exception of Morocco, contain provisions on parallel imports, and the relevant provision in the Morocco FTA reflects a pre-existing provision in Morocco's domestic law.

Our most recent FTAs, those with Morocco and CAFTA, expressly state that nothing in the IP chapters in those agreements affects a country's ability to take measures necessary to protect public health or prevents effective utilization of the agreement reached in the WTO last year to ensure that developing countries that lack pharmaceutical manufacturing capacity may import drugs.

Jakkrit turns next to investor-state dispute settlement, arguing that countries will be exposed to monetary damages if they adopt safety regulations, including those related to GM foods. However, legitimate, non-discriminatory safety regulations are entirely appropriate and consistent with U.S. FTAs, and it is hard to imagine a case where they would give rise to liability.

Jakkrit's allegations with respect to copyright protections are similarly unsubstantiated. FTAs do not allow copyright owners "to extend control over access to works that have fallen into the public domain." In fact, the FTA text makes explicit that works in the public domain stay there.

Jakkrit seems to believe that copyright piracy should be allowed, even encouraged. How else to explain his criticism of rules that prevent circumvention of technology designed to prevent illicit copying? He asserts that these rules will "affect the public right of fair use." To the contrary, the FTAs provide numerous explicit exceptions and permit governments to make further exceptions to allow circumvention to facilitate fair uses.

Finally, Jakkrit asserts that the "worst change is the demand for rights against temporary reproduction." Protection of temporary copies did not begin with FTAs—the Berne Convention already requires such protection. Furthermore, the FTA explicitly allows countries to continue to make Berne-compatible exceptions for temporary copies, including for fair use. Protection of temporary copies has not hindered the tremendous growth of the Internet. In fact, failing to protect temporary copies would create an enormous loophole for Internet piracy.

In sum, Jakkrit's attack on U.S. FTAs is riddled with inaccuracies and fails to recognize the underlying benefits of IP protection. It is difficult to see how such misinformation benefits the developing world that Jakkrit purports to protect.

The FTAA and the World

By David Fleshler
Sun-Sentinel (Fort Lauderdale, FL), November 16, 2003

In the world of trade negotiators who spend their days discussing tariffs, subsidies, and current accounts, environmental issues rarely play a major role. And when they come up, they're often treated as protectionism in veiled form—as they were in 1998 when an international trade panel ruled against a U.S. ban on shrimp imports from nets that drowned sea turtles.

At the Free Trade Area of the Americas talks in Miami this week, the environment will have a place at the table, although it will be a limited place. When Congress gave the Bush administration wide authority to negotiate the agreement, it required the inclusion of provisions to protect the environment. But Brazil and other developing countries oppose environmental safeguards as "green protectionism," an attempt by wealthy countries to maintain the lead they developed over the past 100 years by operating their own industries without strong pollution controls.

Still, many analysts expect the language in the agreement to be modeled on a recent trade pact between the United States and Chile, which provides for penalties if either country lowers environmental standards to attract jobs. Environmentalists say such protections will mean little in countries whose environmental laws and enforcement mechanisms already are much weaker than those of rich countries. They say the FTAA talks represent the latest step in the drive by corporations and their pro-business allies in government to strip nations of the power to protect their air, water, and land.

"These negotiations are developing new rules that shift the balance of power toward private property rights and away from the ability of governments to legislate in favor of the public interest," said Dan Seligman, trade program director for the Sierra Club.

Like the debate over the FTAA and jobs, the environmental debate is rooted in the experience of the North American Free Trade Agreement. After NAFTA was ratified, more U.S. companies moved their factories over the border, where they contributed to a major air pollution problem. But many experts say this transfer of factories wasn't the most significant environmental impact of NAFTA. More important was a rule that allows foreign investors to challenge other countries' decisions on the environment and other issues, a rule that is likely to be replicated under the FTAA.

About the Agreement

What: The Free Trade Area of the Americas pact would slash barriers to trade and create the world's largest free trade zone, encompassing more than 800 million people from Alaska to Argentina.

It would expand on the North American Free Trade Agreement among the United States, Canada, and Mexico.

Who: 34 nations in the Americas—all but Cuba.

When: Proposed for 2005, after a decade of negotiations.

Where: Site for the headquarters is up for grabs. Miami is vying against at least eight other cities, including Atlanta and Panama City, Panama.

Why: Proponents say the FTAA would boost economic growth, ease poverty, and make governments more accountable. Critics say big nations would swamp the small and multinational corporations would gain most.

"Yes, some businesses relocate because of trade agreements—but more often this is to find low-wage havens, not pollution havens," said Eric Dannenmaier, director of the Tulane University Institute for Environmental Law and Policy, who has been an environmental advisor to the governments of Argentina, Chile, Bolivia, Peru, and Ecuador. "And yes, as businesses find low-wage havens, pollution intensity increases in countries less equipped to handle the load. Yet the real environmental problems with trade agreements are far more complex and subtle."

NAFTA allows companies or individual investors to file claims for damages over any action by a national or local government that deprives them of the value of their investment. The complaints go to a three-member trade panel whose hearings are closed to the public.

For example, Metalclad Corp., a U.S. company, filed a claim after a local government in Mexico rejected its request for a permit for a hazardous waste landfill. Metalclad won damages of $16.7 million. And last August, after California passed a tough mine cleanup law, the Canadian company Glamis Gold Ltd. filed a claim for damages with a NAFTA trade panel. Glamis said the new law destroyed the value of its mining concession on 1,500 square miles of desert. That case is pending.

So far, just four claims have resulted in money judgments. And the total amount awarded—about $28 million to all four successful claimants—is modest compared to the scope of trade among the three countries. But legal experts say the threat of an investor-protection suit could have a chilling effect on proposals to strengthen environmental laws in the United States and the other countries in the agreement. And they say it's unfair and undemocratic for companies to be able to challenge such laws in closed tribunals.

"It is fundamentally wrong for the validity of important national and international environmental measures to be decided in closed private arbitration proceedings that take place outside the jurisdiction where such measures take effect and outside of any meaningful public review or awareness," wrote attorneys Stephen L. Kass and Jean M. McCarroll in the *New York Law Journal.*

The FTAA draft provides for similar panels, and environmentalists fear it could be used to circumvent the laws of the United States and those of other countries. For example, the Sierra Club says the Venezuelan oil company Citgo, which sells gasoline in the United States, could challenge U.S. air and water standards. Or U.S. companies could file a claim against the Brazilian government over the right to operate gold mines in the Amazon.

FTAA supporters say such investor-protection rules are necessary to protect U.S. investors in countries with less-than-reliable legal systems. "In many countries, the same standards of rule of law and transparent administration are not universally adhered to," said John Murphy, vice president for Western Hemisphere affairs at the U.S. Chamber of Commerce. "It's very useful to have recourse to an international arbitrator."

And some experts say increased foreign trade can improve environmental performance because it thrusts corporations into the glare of international publicity. No one wants to face the sort of boycotts over labor and environmental practices that hit Nike, Exxon, and The Gap. So a Brazilian shoe company, for example, would acquire a strong interest in improving its standards if it wanted to export to the United States.

"Once you're competing in the international market, the demand side has a very high environmental concern," said Ronaldo Seroa de Motta, coordinator of regulation studies at the Institute for Applied Economics in Brasilia. "They're not doing that for the citizens of Brazil, they're doing that for the international market. They're doing it for clean propaganda for the outside world."

The impact of increased trade and investment also depends on how well a country can enforce environmental standards. Among the least prepared are Guatemala, Honduras, Nicaragua, Panama, and Ecuador, said Robin Rosenberg, deputy director of the University of Miami's North-South Center. These countries lack strong environmental agencies, databases, inspection systems, and courts that will stand up to the money and influence of big polluters, he said. And even countries with adequate laws may not enforce them.

"Is El Salvador going to close down a tanning factory that's polluting a river?" Rosenberg asked. "They need the jobs. And how many inspectors do they have? And is the court system going to back them up?"

And the FTAA could have a profound impact on South America's vast Amazon rain forest, which extends into eight countries. The forest is home to jaguars, scarlet macaws, howler monkeys, and more than 1,000 species of butterflies. It is also home to deposits of gold, nickel, oil, and natural gas, and environmentalists fear that the FTAA will encourage more companies to go after them.

"I think you will create the climate for increased natural-resource extraction, with governments trying to link their energy infrastructure," said Atossa Soltani, executive director of Amazon Watch. "What we fear is there will be less scrutiny and less intervention by civil society."

Leadership

The talks are organized into nine groups that negotiate on separate issues. Here's a look at the groups, which country chairs each, and the issues.

Market Access
- *Chair:* Colombia
- *Aim:* Phase out tariff and non-tariff barriers
- *Challenge:* Some see tough U.S. security rules, post 9-11, as non-tariff barriers.

Agriculture
- *Chair:* Uruguay
- *Aim:* End export subsidies; address quotas and other distortions in farm trade
- *Challenge:* U.S. wants farm subsidies to be resolved in world trade talks, not FTAA.

Investment
- *Chair:* Panama
- *Aim:* Develop rules to promote investment

Challenge: Do broad investor protections restrict government's powers to make local laws?

Intellectual Property Rights
- *Chair:* Dominican Republic
- *Aim:* Boost protections on copyrights, patents, and other intellectual property
- *Challenge:* Will protecting drug patents make some drugs unaffordable for poor countries?

Services
- *Chair:* Caribbean Community
- *Aim:* Liberalize trade in services from banking to insurance
- *Challenge:* Will broad protections give an edge to the more developed, larger U.S. service sector?

Government Procurement
- *Chair:* Costa Rica
- *Aim:* Expand access to government contracts
- *Challenge:* Brazil suggests topic be resolved in world trade talks, not FTAA.
- *Challenge:* U.S. wants topic resolved in world trade talks, not FTAA.

Subsidies, Anti-dumping Policies
- *Chair:* Argentina
- *Aim:* Improve application of trade remedy laws
- *Challenge:* U.S. wants topic resolved in world trade talks, not FTAA.

Dispute Settlement
- *Chair:* Canada
- *Aim:* Set up ways to resolve FTAA disagreements
- *Challenge:* Deciding who should judge and how to structure panels resolving disputes.

Competition Policy
- *Chair:* Peru
- *Aim:* Set antitrust and other competition rules
- *Challenge:* Whose rules should define when mergers may be monopolies?

Why Are Some Trade Agreements "Greener" Than Others?

BY VEENA DUBAL ET AL.
EARTH ISLAND JOURNAL, WINTER 2001–2002

The North American Free Trade Agreement (NAFTA) and the European Union (EU) have done much towards erasing borders and boundaries between nations in the name of free trade. This movement towards a new global era, however, raises concerns on the environmental front. An examination of two toxic disposal controversies—one in Mexico and one in Greece—serves to illuminate NAFTA's and the EU's significantly different takes on environmental regulation.

NAFTA Dumps on Mexico

Concerns about NAFTA and toxic dumping are twofold. The most obvious problem is one of increased waste production with decreased accountability. Glaring examples can be seen in the industrialized maquiladora border region, where Mexican factories produce goods for U.S. consumption with significantly less regulation than north of the border.

In theory, all waste generated from materials in these factories must be returned to the country from which the raw materials originated, a requirement stemming from Article 55 of the Mexican Environmental General Law and the 1983 La Paz Agreement.

Indeed, thousands of tons of hazardous waste are returned to the U.S. each year, mostly to California and Texas. Much of this waste, however, never makes it over the border and is illegally dumped, creating serious health and environmental risks.

The current debate regarding NAFTA and hazardous waste has focused on local sovereignty rather than unregulated production. Mexico produces an estimated 10 million tons of hazardous waste annually. According to Mexico's National Ecological Institute (INE), only 12 percent is ultimately processed in a legitimate manner, with the rest illegally finding its way into municipal drainage systems, landfills, rivers, or abandoned lots.

Mexico possesses only one officially licensed disposal plant. Until more are constructed, any increased regulations relating to hazardous waste disposal will be rendered irrelevant.

In January 1993, the Delaware-based Metalclad Corp. sought to capitalize on this opportunity by purchasing a chunk of land near the city of Guadalcazur as the site of a hazardous waste landfill. The company was issued an INE permit, which authorized the expansion of annual processing capacity to 360,000 tons within two years. But as Metalclad proceeded with investment and development, opposition mounted. Before the plant could officially open in 1995, it was shut down by protests.

Metalclad was forced to abandon its assets, and insult was added to injury in 1997, when the departing state governor declared the plant property to be in the confines of a newly established ecological preserve.

Instead of seeking compensation in a Mexican court, Metalclad demanded arbitration under NAFTA's Chapter 11, a controversial provision that allows investors to sue foreign governments. Metalclad argued that under NAFTA, Mexico was responsible for the conduct of its political subdivisions.

In August 2000, a three-man NAFTA dispute tribunal met in secret and found in favor of Metalclad. The panel (which is not required to provide any public record of its deliberations) ruled that NAFTA's requirements for "fair and equitable treatment" of investments had been violated and that failure to allow construction of the plant was "tantamount to expropriation without compensation."

Furthermore, the tribunal found that the Mexican government itself had "failed to ensure a transparent and predictable framework for Metalclad's business planning and investment." Mexico was ordered to pay Metalclad $16.5 million (plus interest) in damages.

What makes the Metalclad ruling particularly disturbing is that the arbitration panel ruled that the decision to operate hazardous waste processing plants rested solely in the hands of the Mexican federal government. State and municipal environmental concerns were characterized as "incidental interference with the use of property."

In an October 27, 2000, *New York Law Journal* essay, Stephen L. Kass and Jean M. McCarroll note that the Metalclad decision "caused concern among environmentalists in all three NAFTA countries . . . because of the panel's overly broad language and its apparent downgrading of 'environmental concerns' that conflict with investors' expectations."

With the support of the Canadian provinces of Ottawa and Quebec, as well as the Vancouver City Council, Mexico appealed the tribunal's decision in a Vancouver high court. This marked the first time a NAFTA-related decision had been challenged.

On May 7, 2001, in a mixed ruling, the court ordered Mexico to pay Metalclad damages but scolded the three-man tribunal for going "too far" in interpreting how much protection from government policy NAFTA grants to private companies.

Metalclad Chief Financial Officer Anthony Dabbene called the court's decision a loss for his company. "Mexico won, in that Chapter 11 can't hurt them as much anymore," Dabbene stated. "Our case has shown it is almost frivolous to pursue your rights." Dabbene now doubts that Metalclad will ever recoup its estimated $20 million investment.

> *All these post-NAFTA initiatives suffer from governmental neglect.*

NAFTA's Regulatory Process

The NAFTA environmental regime's capacity to cope with trade-related challenges suffers from fundamental impediments. Under NAFTA, domestic environmental laws should not discriminate against trade; thus NAFTA's dispute settlement provisions allow firms to challenge environmental regulations. Since these rules obligate governments to compensate investors for regulations that expropriate an investor's future property, states and provinces may retreat from imposing tough environmental regulations out of the fear of penalization.

Flaws in procedures and programs also impair NAFTA's environmental institutions. Restrictions on Commission for Environmental Cooperation's (CEC) autonomy, problems with its citizen submission, and government-to-government dispute resolution processes are hindrances to its effectiveness. The government of Mexico, for example, has vowed to withhold its support for CEC programs contingent on external approval of the commission's projects.

Under the North American Agreement on Environmental Cooperation's (NAAEC) Articles 14 and 15, citizens are allowed to instigate investigations of alleged non-enforcement of domestic environmental laws. Unfortunately, these citizen-initiated complaints face numerous procedural hurdles and may be terminated by the commission. Rules of procedure have not yet been established for resolving government-to-government disputes under NAAEC's Chapter V—a process that could actually result in penalties—rendering this highly publicized provision virtually toothless.

The Border XXI Program, which shoulders the burden of border area environmental management, has generated some useful initiatives, with 127 projects currently on its docket. Yet Border XXI remains a morass of programs dominated by federal agencies on each side of the border. Projects are moving in haphazard fashion and are contingent on available funds.

All these post-NAFTA initiatives suffer from governmental neglect. None have been adequately funded. The CEC has limped along on $9 million annually (down from the $15 million originally promised). CEC's U.S. staffing is the most inadequate of the three governments.

The Border Environmental Cooperation Commission's operating fund has been in jeopardy from the start. Financing for its certified projects through the Environmental Protection Agency (EPA) and North American Development Bank (NADBank) is also threatened.

Holding Greece Accountable

The European Union (EU) offers an alternate example of environmental regulation in a regional trade organization. The EU's April 7, 2000, decision to fine Greece highlights the contrast between European and North American trade regimes, their institutionalized environmental protections, and the corresponding environmental enforcement efforts.

Greece was the first nation to be fined under Article 171 of the European Community Treaty, which gives the Court of Justice the right to fine nations delinquent in establishing firm plans for waste disposal. Greece has allowed toxic dumping to continue on the island of Crete despite charges from the local community that the pollution was damaging the environment.

The waste, which was being dumped at the tip of the Kouroupitos River near the city of Chania, came from hospitals, common sewage, and industrial sources. Unable to dispose of or recycle the waste, Greece was in violation of a 1981 directive requiring that dangerous waste be disposed of "without endangering human health or the environment."

The Commission of the European Communities, a region-wide oversight board, challenged the Greek government for not adequately protecting its citizens from health and environmental risks. The fact that the Greek government could not find a site for the waste disposal facility was ruled irrelevant by the Court of Justice because treaty obligations were binding regardless of internal conditions.

"Upward Harmonization"

The directive's sweeping nature provides an example of "upward harmonization" in environmental standards. The EU provides its member states with a right to ban imports from other member states that do not reach domestic levels of health, safety, or environmental protection. In order to continue the free exchange of trade within this context, the EU has engaged in a massive exercise to gradually harmonize member states' protection by raising them all to an equal level.

The EU's firm response to the waste problem surprised Greece, and it has cautioned the rest of Europe against violating EU treaties. The fines in Greece have reverberated throughout Europe, causing EU members and prospective members to consider their own shortcomings in abiding by environmental regulations.

The industrial waste problem remains unsolved and no comprehensive waste disposal plan exists. The Greek government now makes monthly payments of 20,000 euros ($17,491) to the European Union for each day that it infringes on the environmental and health integrity of the Chania region with illegally dumped waste.

The fines levied against Greece illustrate a concern for protection of the environment throughout EU territory—concerns often neglected in traditional trade treaties.

While NAFTA regulations have served only to maintain (or even degrade) domestic environmental protection, the EU's upward harmonization has maintained the high standards in its greenest nations—like Germany. EU landfill regulations are only one example of strict regulations typical of Germany's legislation that were instituted throughout the EU in order to raise every member state to an equal level.

The landfill legislation is a revealing example of the overall trend of strong EU environmental policy. In marked contrast to NAFTA's tacked-on environmental protections, the EU's trade-environment rules are well developed and environment-friendly.

There are several explanations for this general policy of upward harmonization: the large influence of green-friendly Germany over EU policy; the centralized legislative control of the European Parliament; and the expansive interpretation by the European Court of Justice of the "least trade-restrictive means necessary" clause of trade block treaties.

Germany's influence is the result of the EU's use of qualified majority voting (QMV) and the German economy's large market power. QMV is a form of voting that grants representation to each member state on a population-weighted basis, rather than giving each member nation one representative. Therefore, the use of QMV in the EU guarantees Germany considerable sway because it has the largest population of any EU member state. Because of its rich markets, Germany also has the ability to threaten or encourage poorer member nations into agreeing to higher regulation standards.

During the mid-'90s debates over auto-emissions standards, for instance, Germany repeatedly threatened to shut its markets to automobiles that did not meet German emission standards, which would have been disastrous for outside car companies. Germany would only accept imported cars if the EU significantly strengthened its standards. Under this pressure, the EU eventually did legislate tougher auto regulations.

With Germany's almost unparalleled levels of environmental protection and the domestic influence of the German Green Party, German leadership in the EU has given a distinct green tinge to the block's policies. Germany's insistence on high levels of environmental protection has spread throughout EU member states.

This push for environmental protection is given added weight because, unlike NAFTA regulations, EU law enjoys unqualified supremacy in all member states. This gives the EU Parliament in Brussels the ability to legislate environmental standards that must be enforced by the courts of all member nations—even if the national legislature is unwilling to pass similar domestic regulation.

NAFTA was not designed to legislate new standards. NAFTA regulations only have the ability to *tear down* national legislation to a uniformly low level through Chapter 11 court cases. The EU's legislative authority, on the other hand, allows it to uniformly *raise* European environmental standards.

Examining the sources of environmental protection within the EU indicates that the further development of environment-friendly trade can only take place along regional paths. In a small enough area, nations that are strong proponents of environmental protection can spread their influence to "green" trade treaties and pull other nations' standards up.

Looking ahead, the Free Trade Agreement of the Americas (FTAA) poses additional dangers. The FTAA draft, as it now stands, contains no safeguards for the environment. It is a vital time to look back at what has and has not worked in the examples of NAFTA and the EU in order to increase awareness of the environmental issues that can and will affect all of us in the years to come.

Paying for NAFTA

By Kevin P. Gallagher
NACLA Report on the Americas, July/August 2004

As many nations now seek deeper integration into the world economy through such fora as the Free Trade Area of the Americas or the World Trade Organization, they would do well to consider Mexico's experience. The Mexican economy, which successive governments have been liberalizing since 1985, is now one of the most open in the world. However, the country is also a showcase highlighting the environmental costs that can accompany trade-led growth when the proper regulatory institutions are absent.

During negotiations for the North American Free Trade Agreement (NAFTA), proponents of the deal asserted free trade would automatically lead to improved environmental conditions in its member countries, particularly Mexico. By increasing incomes, they argued, free trade would produce the funds to underwrite environmental improvement. In actuality, environmental degradation has increased. Furthermore, statistics from Mexico's National Institute for Statistics, Geography, and Information Systems (INEGI) document how this environmental degradation has undermined the benefits of Mexico's trade-led economic growth.

According to INEGI, between 1985 and 1999 rural soil erosion grew by 89 percent, municipal solid waste production by 108 percent, water pollution by 29 percent, and urban air pollution by 97 percent. The results have been costly. INEGI studies estimate the financial costs of environmental degradation at 10 percent of GDP from 1988 to 1999, an average of $36 billion in damage each year— $47 billion for 1999. The cost of this destruction overwhelms the pace of economic growth, which has hovered at an average of 2.5 percent annually over the same period, or $14 billion per year.

Costly environmental degradation is occurring because the proper mechanisms were not put in place to help Mexico manage its economic growth in an environmentally sustainable manner. This is unfortunate because in the years leading up to the signing of NAFTA, Mexico had begun to show environmental improvements. Spending on environmental protection was on the rise and Mexico had implemented a much-needed industrial environmental inspection program. With the onset of NAFTA, however, and its consequent fiscal and financial woes, attention to the environment nosedived. According to INEGI, since 1994 real spending on environmental protection declined by 45 percent. Even at their highest lev-

NACLA Report on the Americas; Vol. 38:1, p 47. Copyright 2004 by the North American Congress on Latin America, 38 Greene St., New York, NY 10013. *www.nacla.org*

els, allocations for environmental protection were paltry in comparison to Mexico's counterparts in the Organization for Economic Cooperation and Development (OECD); as a percentage of GDP, they were only a fifth the size of those made by other OECD nations.

NAFTA's "Environmental Side Agreement" created institutions, including the North American Commission for Environmental Cooperation (NACEC), to monitor and ensure that member states follow environmental regulations. They have set some important precedents, but they are not equipped to deal with Mexico's environmental crisis. At most, Mexico receives only a third of the NACEC's $9 million annual budget. NACEC has been effective in carrying out its limited mandate, enabling citizen groups to monitor environmental progress and convening cross-national information sharing and research efforts in North America. But the $3 million budgeted for Mexico is dwarfed by the country's budget shortfalls and is buried beneath environmental degradation's $36 billion price tag. Mexico's environmental crisis clearly underscores the fact that, without the proper environmental policies in place, the environmental consequences of trade-led growth could undermine the very goals of economic integration.

Truckers Worry About Equal Requirements

By Richard Benke
Associated Press, June 8, 2004

Truckers, motor transport inspectors, even the governor of New Mexico expressed misgivings about a U.S. Supreme Court ruling that suddenly opens U.S. highways to Mexico's trucks.

More than 30,000 commercial trucks a year cross into New Mexico from Mexico, U.S. customs officials said, and more than 600,000 a year cross into neighboring El Paso, Texas. But until the high court's unanimous ruling Monday, those trucks were restricted to a limited area along the border, where they could deposit their cargo in warehouses and storage yards. U.S. carriers would finish their trips.

That, according to the Bush administration, was a violation of the North American Free Trade Agreement. The Clinton administration had tried to hold off free access for the trucks, arguing an environmental assessment was necessary. President Bush sought to open the gates in 2002, but encountered lawsuits.

Supreme Court Justice Clarence Thomas, writing the ruling issued Monday, said it was the president's call.

New Mexico Gov. Bill Richardson said he's concerned that the border states' motor transport standards may be lost in the NAFTA push.

"I have concerns with the public safety, health, and air quality implications that these Mexican trucks may present in a border state like New Mexico," Richardson said in a statement Monday. "Within New Mexico's border region there are already two areas where air pollutants like ozone and dust are above federal standards. I am concerned that this decision could further degrade air quality and expose border state residents to harmful pollution."

Royal Jones, president of Las Cruces–based Mesilla Valley Transport Service Inc., worried that Mexican truckers might gain a competitive advantage by not having to comply with all the regulations U.S. companies do. His company routes 650 trucks nationwide.

"They need to meet the same standards that we have to meet. That's only fair," Jones said.

Whatever regulations are imposed, he said, the U.S. Department of Transportation still may not equalize the Mexican trucker's burden.

If the advantages remained unequal, he said, he just might move his company to Mexico.

Lt. Bryan Credeur, who inspects trucks at the New Mexico Motor Transport Division scales in Anthony, N.M., sees Mexican trucks coming in from Santa Teresa and El Paso.

Most U.S. Department of Transportation rules that apply to all truckers, foreign or domestic, will continue to apply, he said, including the

Upgrading Mexican trucks may cost more than their owners are ready to pay

$750,000 worth of liability insurance that is required, as well as standards for brakes, tires, and background checks on every prospective driver.

"They are held to the same standards that the American companies are," he said.

Upgrading Mexican trucks may cost more than their owners are ready to pay, so they may not come at once in large numbers, said Jim Creek, operations manager for the New Mexico Border Authority.

"It will take a significant investment on their part (to be competitive)," Creek said.

And some Mexican companies have reciprocal agreements with U.S. companies to carry cargo into the depths of Mexico while U.S. drivers truck Mexican cargo throughout the United States, Jones said.

"I have a Mexican carrier who I have an agreement with," he said. "That's been a great deal, and I think a lot of people will continue to do it that way."

Added Creek: "What we see here now at least is the Mexican trucking industry at the border is not equipped for the long haul."

Credeur said he has watched Mexican trucking come more into compliance with U.S. standards in the 11 years of NAFTA—"from 75 percent of trucks taken out of service to about 25 percent," which he said echoes the average for U.S. truckers.

Jones said he cannot hire a driver with a DWI on his record. How, he asks, will U.S. inspectors know a driving record is as it claims to be?

Credeur said U.S. inspectors will have to take on faith that such records are accurate.

What about the law requiring all truckers to be fluent in English, Jones wanted to know.

"Is that rule going to be overwritten now too?" he asked.

Credeur, who was asked that question a few moments later, declined comment.

But he said he does have some law enforcement concerns in the wake of Sept. 11, 2001, and the advent of homeland security. He said he's grateful that the trucks have to clear customs before coming in for inspection at his scales.

"I would expect a larger number of Mexican carriers to come through once this is implemented," Credeur said. "It could happen slowly, or it could happen overnight."

He said he was surprised how little warning there was before the Supreme Court ruling came down. But he said the industry knew something like it might one day arrive.

"We have taken tentative steps to anticipate and meet this," Credeur said. "I think we all felt it was going to be an eventuality. I think a lot of people were anticipating this going on a little longer. Now it remains to be seen what the next step is."

Richardson said he expressed similar concerns in writing to the U.S. Department of Transportation last November. He said New Mexico will continue monitoring for pollution.

Raul Garcia, risk management director for Mesilla Valley Transport, worried that there might be a "snowball effect" at the border if it happened too fast.

"We've got to make sure that by solving one problem we don't create 20 more," he said.

Workers Say Rights Denied As Firms Threaten to Pull Out

By Susan Ferriss
Cox News Service, October 30, 2003

Martin Zacatzi Tequextle can recite the names of trendy jeans like an American mall rat: "Tommy Hilfiger, Calvin Klein, Levi's, Guess."

He ought to know. Before he was fired this summer, Zacatzi alleges that he and 1,300 other employees at a textile factory in southern Mexico were forced to sew together thousands of jeans a day with little or no overtime compensation to augment base wages of little more than $1 an hour.

Sometimes they were ordered to sew from 8 A.M. on Fridays until 4 A.M. on Saturdays, say former and current workers at the factory in Ajalpan, a small town in Puebla state about 175 miles southeast of Mexico City.

The factory is co-owned by Tarrant Apparel Group of Los Angeles and wealthy Mexican textile magnate Kamel Nacif, who has made headlines in Las Vegas for high-stakes gambling. Workers here have dubbed Nacif "The Denim King," because he owns multiple factories, known in Spanish as maquiladoras, that assemble jeans.

Labor activists on both sides of the border regard the Tarrant Mexico dispute as the latest test case for Mexico's willingness to enforce maquiladora workers' rights. Allegations of sweatshop conditions are also putting pressure on big-name U.S. brands to oblige foreign suppliers to abide by codes of conduct and local labor laws.

In the past, workers at Mexican maquiladoras have been subjected to forced pregnancy testing and other invasions of privacy, or fired for protesting abuses, in spite of Mexican labor laws that appear generous to employees on paper.

In today's Mexico, workers who try to exercise their rights are feeling the squeeze of global competition.

At the Ajalpan factory, some of the workers say supervisors are warning them to acquiesce to excessive demands that they work harder and faster—or else the U.S. companies that once flocked to Mexico will go to China, where workers earn even less.

Because import tariffs were lowered by the 1994 North American Free Trade Agreement, NAFTA, Mexico's textile maquiladoras mushroomed to 1,092 factories by 2001. By June of this year, because of the U.S. economic slowdown and an increase in textile assembly in China, Central America, and other poorer regions, that number had fallen to 796.

The threat of China "is used a lot as a pretext now at factories," said Zacatzi. "China needs work. It's got a huge population. But Mexico needs work, too."

The 37-year-old says he turned down nearly $3,000 in severance pay offered by Tarrant, opting instead to challenge his sudden dismissal before a state labor board.

"We're not against transnational companies coming to our country. We welcome them. But we want people to know that Mexican workers are being exploited," added Zacatzi.

The dispute at Tarrant Mexico began in June, when about 800 workers staged a *Norma Rae*–style work stoppage. Then they gathered about 750 signatures demanding they be allowed to form an independent union, rare in Mexico because unions were for so many decades controlled by Mexico's former one-party government.

"We want people to know that Mexican workers are being exploited."—Martin Zacatzi
Tequextle, a Mexican textile worker

The employees claim they collected enough signatures to require the state labor board to approve their union. But in early October, the board rejected the petition on grounds the employees believe were flimsy excuses to thwart them and protect the influential Nacif.

One of the reasons the board cited for the rejection: The name of a woman union supporter was listed as "Maria" on one document and "Maura" on another.

Since their work stoppage, employees also say, Tarrant has fired workers in waves, starting with all the leaders of the union drive, including Zacatzi. So far, more than 300 employees have been dismissed.

"There are imbalances of power in every country, but Mexico is pretty extreme," said Scott Nova, executive director of the Washington, D.C.–based Workers Rights Consortium, a non-profit group that investigates sweatshop allegations and is respected by big companies like Levi Strauss & Co.

Nova's group produced a damning report on the Ajalpan plant, and in September sent copies to Levi Strauss and Tommy Hilfiger, two top Tarrant Mexico customers.

Levi Strauss asked Tarrant Mexico to become more active in addressing workers' grievances and allow an independent auditor to investigate allegations of abuses at the plant. Tarrant refused, angering Levi Strauss.

"To our surprise, the company was not willing to work with us. It's a very rare case," said Michael Kobori, director of Levi Strauss' "global code of conduct" section, which oversees internal labor standards at its suppliers' plants.

In September, Levi Strauss stopped placing orders with Tarrant and wrote a letter to Puebla's governor, Melquiades Morales Flores, urging him to uphold Mexico's labor laws.

Also in September, a U.S. college group called United Students Against Sweatshops filed a complaint related to the Tarrant Mexico dispute before a three-country labor review board established by NAFTA. Along with Mexican activists, the students accused Mexico's government of failing to uphold its own laws.

Blame for the Tarrant plant dispute ricochets among the players at the top of the production chain.

Nacif's office in Mexico City referred calls to Jorge Echeverria, a plant spokesman, who said the 300 layoffs were necessary because companies like Levi Strauss don't want to pay the factory enough. Because of the economy, he added, production at Tarrant's various Mexican plants has fallen by 50 percent or more.

Echeverria called the union supporters who were fired "bad for Mexico" because their actions were costing the company work.

"Don't you know the United States doesn't buy from us anymore?" he said. "That you buy everything from China now? Then you send people down here to dare to investigate human rights abuses."

Tarrant, he said, rejected Levi Strauss' business because it wanted to offer "hunger wages."

Levi Strauss' policy is not to discuss details of specific transactions.

But in a statement, the company said: "We can tell you that we have reached mutually satisfactory agreements with over 500 contractors throughout the world who are willing to meet our requirements for service, time, and cost of production, as well as meeting our code of conduct requirements."

Patrick Chow, Tarrant chief financial officer in Los Angeles, [California,] also accused Levi Strauss of failing to offer enough money. As for Levi Strauss' request for an audit, he said, "Why should we let them in? They decided not to do business with us."

The Ajalpan plant is currently churning out Express jeans for The Limited, a chain clothing retailer that caters to young U.S. women. The brand responded to inquiries about its position on the Tarrant dispute with a statement: "Limited Brands holds its employees, suppliers, and vendors strictly accountable for compliance with all applicable laws and our own business policies, including those relating to labor standards."

Representatives of Puebla's labor board did not return repeated phone calls for comment.

The Tarrant Mexico conflict is reminiscent of a fight nearby at Puebla's Mexmode factory, a Korean-owned plant where employees rose up in 2001 to demand a union and to protest abuses.

After the intervention of the company's major buyer, Nike, and United Students Against Sweatshops, the independent union was installed.

Today, more than 700 assembly workers at sewing machines piece together T-shirts and sweatshirts emblazoned with Nike, Disney, or the names of U.S. college sports teams. And every Monday, manager Steve Kim or others sit down with union leaders to talk about problems.

"The union is like the face of the company now," Kim said.

Mexmode's workers are happier, said union leader Josefina Perez. The wages still aren't high enough to dissuade some from joining the trail of illegal immigrants to the United States that flows heavily out of Puebla. But many feel they have a stake in the company now, and for the first time in several years, Kim said, he expects to make a profit next year.

What happens at the Tarrant Mexico plant, U.S. activists say, depends on whether brands like The Limited will follow Nike and Levi Strauss and use their leverage to pressure the company.

In contrast to Levi Strauss, which took a public stand, Tommy Hilfiger pulled out quietly in what activists call a "cut and run," said United Students Against Sweatshops national organizer Ben McKean.

"The answer is not to drop the company like a hot potato," McKean said. "If a brand leaves every time workers try to organize an independent union, there will never be workers' rights in Mexico.

Women's Edge Coalition's New Study Demonstrates that NAFTA Has Hurt Poor Women in Mexico, FTAA Will Make It Worse

U.S. NEWSWIRE, NOVEMBER 18, 2003

The Women's Edge Coalition, a nonpartisan organization that advocates international economic policies and human rights that support poor women worldwide, today announced it has completed its groundbreaking case study to analyze the impact of the North American Free Trade Agreement (NAFTA) and future impact of the Free Trade Area of the Americas (FTAA) on Mexico's poor farmers, with a particular emphasis on women.

To conduct the analysis, the organization used its Trade Impact Review (TIR), a framework developed to determine the positive and negative consequences a trade agreement will have before it is signed.

Women and Trade

Over the last several years, the Women's Edge Coalition has become increasingly concerned with how U.S. trade policies affect women and the poor in developing countries. Currently trade is considered to be gender-neutral, when in fact, trade agreements produce changes that affect men and women differently.

"Women are being abandoned, left behind by trade agreements," said Ritu Sharma, co-founder and executive director, Women's Edge Coalition. "They are the majority of the poor in this world, and if trade is supposed to help the poor, it has got to help women."

NAFTA's Impacts on Women Uncovered

- Poverty increased by 50 percent for women-headed households since the implementation of NAFTA. In contrast, poverty for men decreased by 5.4 percent.

- Women, more than men, benefited from non-traditional agricultural jobs, gaining 83 percent of the new jobs created in the sector. But, for the same job in the non-traditional agriculture sector, women earn 25 to 30 percent less than men. This explains why women gained more jobs in this sector—they are cheaper labor.

- 300,000 women farmers lost jobs, and these farmers are the poorest of the poor and have the worst land to farm.

- Of women farmers in Mexico, only three percent have more than 10 hectares of land, much less than men. Women are the poorest farmers in Mexico.

- Wages for women and men both dropped after NAFTA. However, women's wages were lower than men's to begin with. Therefore, the drop in women's wages caused many to go into much deeper poverty than men.

- Due to NAFTA, Mexico changed its land ownership laws to favor individual property rights. This hurt women who previously had communal rights to farm land because when land becomes titled, it almost automatically goes to men.

NAFTA's Impacts on the Rural Poor

NAFTA was created with the explicit goal of reducing poverty in Mexico by creating a large, middle-income population in the country. However, the findings clearly demonstrate that goal has not been accomplished—many of Mexico's poor have become poorer. Now NAFTA is the blueprint for the Free Trade Area of the Americas Agreement (FTAA), a trade agreement that will cover the entire Western Hemisphere.

- NAFTA created 5.3 million jobs both in the formal and informal sectors. The TIR uncovered that approximately 36 percent of these jobs were created in the informal sector where workers typically receive no benefits, are not entitled to vacation pay or overtime, and routinely have no contract protections.

- 1.3 million jobs in agriculture were lost in Mexico due to NAFTA (1 million men and 300,000 women). Many that lost their jobs in this sector could not transfer to the newly created jobs due to lack of education.

- Monthly income for self-employed farmers fell from 1,959 pesos a month in 1991 to 228 pesos a month in 2003.

- The quality of living for poor farmers dropped dramatically; there was a 50 percent decline in the basic goods (such as food, clothing, health, education, and housing) that Mexicans could afford to buy between 1990 and 2000, further exacerbating poverty issues for women.

FTAA Forecasting: More Job Losses for the Poor

If the current trend continues with the FTAA, at *best*, over a five-year time period, 350,000 more jobs will be lost in Mexico's agricultural sector and that number could go up to 750,000.

About the Trade Impact Review

If the U.S. and other governments want trade policies to benefit the poor here and abroad, it is critical to conduct a TIR, which does not require extensive time or resources.

By using the TIR, policy makers can either modify a trade agreement so that the poor do not lose their jobs or they can develop U.S. and Mexican assistance programs to help transition the displaced workers to jobs that pay decent, livable wages.

VI. The Future of FTAs and NAFTA

Editor's Introduction

While more than 10 years have passed since NAFTA's inception, the pros and cons of the agreement continue to be debated. In presenting their case against the accord, NAFTA opponents cite job losses, environmental excesses, and human rights abuses; nevertheless, this criticism has not deterred nations worldwide from entering free trade agreements (FTAs) of their own, particularly in Asia and Latin America, as well as the industrialized West. Already ubiquitous, FTAs are expected to become even more common in the future. Mexico currently leads the world with a total of 43 free trade accords; meanwhile, the United States has initiated FTA talks with several Latin American nations, and Canada has indicated its desire to expand NAFTA. With the ascendance of free trade, the significance of NAFTA has only increased: Nations use it as both a model and a cautionary example as they seek to access the benefits of FTAs while minimizing some of the negative side effects. Chapter 6 weighs the future of NAFTA and how FTAs may evolve in the decades to come as nations and regions tailor them to suit their needs.

Despite the current preeminence of free trade, its future is by no means assured. The first article in Chapter 6, Paul Blustein's "Walkout Shadows Free Trade's Future," looks at the potential for a future without global free trade, especially in light of the difficult negotiations at the meeting of the World Trade Organization in Cancún, Mexico, in September 2003. A major obstacle has come from rich and developing countries, who are reluctant to sacrifice lucrative tariffs and subsidies for politically influential industries such as agriculture, textile, and apparel.

The future of NAFTA as it relates to the United States and Canada is the subject of the next article, "North American Partnership Inevitable." This piece by Perrin Beatty discusses the bonds between the two nations and argues that a broader partnership is unavoidable, even in the wake of September 11, when security at the world's longest undefended border has had to be strengthened.

While the framework of NAFTA is frequently employed as a model for other free trade pacts, some countries are starting to use the structure of the European Union (EU) as a blueprint. Indeed, a consortium of South American nations is now debating the formation of a free trade zone in their region. "South American Leaders to Set Goal of EU-like Union," by Tyler Bridges, discusses the implications of such an association in South America.

As more countries open their borders to FTAs, balancing the demands of free trade and local sovereignty has proven a difficult task. California, for instance, in an effort to protect the health of its citizens, ruled a specific carcinogen illegal; the state's decision, in turn, violated terms of the NAFTA agreement and resulted in a suit being filed against California. This incident is one of many that have affected U.S. states as the American government expands trade liberalization and U.S. laws come into conflict with agreements made with their trading partners. The final article in this chapter, "Groups Defend California's Right to Protect Public Health," examines the situation of state sovereignty versus free trade.

Walkout Shadows Free Trade's Future

By Paul Blustein
The Washington Post, September 16, 2003

The walkout staged by some of the world's poorest countries that abruptly ended global trade negotiations in Cancun, Mexico, underscored a bedrock question: After decades of rapidly advancing globalization, do the nations of the world lack the stomach to open their borders further to trade and investment?

The prospect that free trade might be reaching its limits, deeply unsettling to some and cheering to others, arose in the wake of the collapse Sunday of World Trade Organization talks. The Cancun meeting, which was supposed to invigorate negotiations launched two years ago for a new pact to lower trade barriers worldwide, broke down amid accusations by developing nations that rich nations were refusing to offer meaningful concessions, all but dooming chances that agreement will be reached by the self-imposed deadline of Jan. 1, 2005.

Yesterday, officials of the developing countries that had forced the rupture were emphasizing that they were still interested in reaching a deal, and trade experts pointed out that brinkmanship and delays are the norm, not the exception, in global trade rounds. But well before the Cancun meeting, the 148 member nations of the WTO were struggling to reach agreement even on basic procedural issues, and the debacle at Cancun has laid bare the enormous obstacles that must be surmounted for a pact to be concluded.

At bottom, the problem facing the eight-year-old WTO can be blamed on its success—and that of its predecessor organization, the General Agreement on Tariffs and Trade—in sharply reducing trade barriers during the post–World War II era.

After eight rounds of negotiations that slashed tariffs and dismantled other obstacles to the movement of goods and services across borders, the United States and the European Union—the two biggest players in the organization—"essentially have very little to give, except the most politically sensitive areas that have survived the previous rounds," said Jeffrey J. Schott, a trade specialist at the Institute for International Economics. In Europe, the most sensitive area is the highly protected farm sector, and in the

United States, it is not only agriculture but also the textile and apparel industries, where tariffs remain high in part because of the clout those industries wield in Washington.

The Europeans are extremely reluctant to give up subsidies for their farmers. As for the United States, Schott noted, if U.S. Trade Representative Robert B. Zoellick offers major concessions in agriculture and textiles to strike a bargain, "Congress will only accept that if they get a good payoff in return," meaning promises by developing countries to significantly increase access in their markets to foreign goods. But many developing countries indicated at Cancun that they are deeply resistant to exposing their industries further to international competition, "and if you were Bob Zoellick, you'd have to ask, 'Do I want to spend time with these guys who don't seem to want to negotiate?'" Schott said.

If that dynamic persists, globalization, at least in its economic form, appears likely to hit a relatively slow patch for a number of years. That doesn't mean that the world trading system would cease

---

Failing to conclude the WTO negotiations... would mean passing up a major opportunity to expand world trade.

---

to function as it does now; the Geneva-based WTO would continue to police global commerce and adjudicate disputes among member nations. But at the very least, failing to conclude the WTO negotiations, which were launched at Doha, Qatar, in November 2001, would mean passing up a major opportunity to expand world trade—one that, according to the World Bank, could boost global incomes by as much as $500 billion a year, enough to raise 144 million people out of poverty by 2015.

The growing backlash against free trade in rich countries, and parallel trends in the developing world, may make such an outcome inevitable, trade experts said.

"The hemorrhaging of U.S. manufacturing jobs and the persistence of high unemployment have placed Zoellick in a position where he has very little room to maneuver," said Daniel K. Tarullo, who served as President Clinton's international economic adviser. Neither the EU nor the United States seems capable of offering much to the developing countries, he added, because "both are restrained by a lack of political support at home for trade expansion and by the political strength of their farmers."

The gloom among free-trade advocates over the events in Cancun was leavened by the belief that the meeting could ironically spur progress toward a global trade deal by drawing world attention to the issues that were raised by the developing countries—in particular, the $300 billion that rich nations pay in subsidies to their farmers. Those subsidies lead to overproduction of many crops, such as cotton, which are then dumped on global markets, depressing prices and hurting farmers in poor lands.

"It's pretty embarrassing for the United States to be seen in an argument with Benin and Mali, two very poor countries, over cotton subsidies," said Edward Gresser, a trade expert at the Progressive Policy Institute. "In a way, it's nice to see countries like that using the system in the way that it ought to be used."

Poor nations were delighted with the propaganda points they scored, and the unity they maintained, at Cancun. "This is the best thing that has happened to developing nations in a long time. I mean, for heaven's sake, if Africans have to compete with rich nations on the price of exporting a mango or rice or cotton or yogurt, how can we ever work our way out of poverty?" said Lucia Quachey, national president of the Ghana Association of Women Entrepreneurs, based in the country's capital, Accra. "It had to be done. A dramatic stand had to be taken."

But, Gresser warned, "ultimately this could be a hollow victory for them." The only realistic chance for reducing the farm subsidies lies in successful completion of the Doha round, he noted, "and if that doesn't get back on track, what good have they done themselves?"

Agriculture was not the only source of friction at Cancun; in fact, the direct cause of the breakdown was the failure to agree on whether a final pact should include WTO rules, sought by the EU and Japan, in areas not currently covered by the organization such as cross-border investment and antitrust.

Whatever the cause, one of the effects will clearly be an intensified effort by the Bush administration to negotiate bilateral free trade accords with individual countries and groups of countries, similar to the North American Free Trade Agreement. Zoellick recently wrapped up such deals with Chile and Singapore, and he has also launched talks with five Central American countries, Australia, Morocco, and several southern African countries.

French foreign minister Dominique de Villepin warned in a French radio interview against "the temptation" of bilateralism, echoing the widely held concern that such deals can undermine the WTO.

One of the purposes of bilateral pacts is to prod recalcitrant countries to come around in the WTO talks, because they would fear that other nations will gain a competitive edge in the giant U.S. market. But many of the countries with whom Washington is negotiating free trade pacts are among the Group of 22, which played a key role in standing up to the United States and the European Union at Cancun. They include Guatemala, Argentina, Costa Rica, and Brazil.

Underscoring the problems Washington has in pursuing bilateral and regional deals, Roberto Rodriguez, Brazil's agriculture minister, said yesterday that the failure to reach an agreement at Cancun jeopardized not only the WTO round but also the U.S. efforts to negotiate a Free Trade Area of the Americas, which would include all the nations of the Western Hemisphere except Cuba. Brazil, the largest nation in Latin America, has staunchly maintained that it would not join an FTAA without obtaining major concessions from Washington on agriculture subsidies; yet at the same time the United States has insisted that a deal on subsidies can only come as part of a WTO agreement.

A senior U.S. official, briefing reporters yesterday on the condition that she not be named, pointedly emphasized that "we will continue to move ahead on the regional and bilateral level." Although the official emphasized that the administration remains as committed as ever to securing a WTO deal, she acknowledged that Cancun raised serious concerns about the prospects.

"Here's a fact as we come out of Cancun: Bold reform on the global level has been delayed," she said. "For countries like us that have been interested in reducing farm subsidies, in reducing goods barriers, that is now delayed. . . . Now how far does that time frame change? We'll see."

North American Partnership Inevitable

BY PERRIN BEATTY
NATIONAL POST (CANADA), SEPTEMBER 12, 2002

It has been a year now since the world was stunned by the horrific events of Sept. 11. The terrible loss of life, the ugliness of terrorism, and the determination of a nation to overcome their impact have left an imprint on all of us and forever changed Canada–U.S. relations.

The borders crisis spawned by the terrorist attacks forced immediate decisions about a common strategy of border management. It was clear the United States would fortify its perimeter—the issue for Canada was whether we wanted to be on the inside or outside. For the vast majority of Canadians, the decision was straightforward. Hundreds of thousands of Canadian jobs depended on having access to the U.S. market and, while Canada itself was not a primary target for terrorists, it could easily come under attack if it became the weak point in U.S. defences.

Tackling that crisis brought Canadian business together in common purpose through the Coalition for Secure and Trade-Efficient Borders. The private sector united behind the efforts of the Canadian government, which consulted closely with the coalition and acted on its input. In fact, I cannot recall any other instance, during my 21 years as a member of Parliament and Cabinet minister, where Canada's business community came together so immediately on a critical issue, and where our federal government responded so swiftly to its concerns. Both governments are to be commended for their quick and decisive action. They are working not to return to border conditions as they were at 8:30 A.M. on Sept. 11, 2001, but to improve them, resolving problems that were important then but are urgent now.

Not only has the aftermath of Sept. 11 forced Canadians to re-examine whether it is possible to pick and choose when it will be engaged with its next-door neighbour, but it has also elevated the importance of the bilateral relationship on the agendas of both the Canadian and American governments, and drawn the two countries more closely together in foreign policy and security issues. And in Canada, it has put the spotlight firmly on the issue of the North American partnership, starting with closer collaboration between Canada and the United States.

Before Sept. 11, the Canadian government's trade policy consisted of going broader, not deeper. The aim was to develop new markets outside North America by diversifying through a Free Trade Area of the Americas and other bilateral agreements, while also working to reduce barriers to Canadian exports at the World Trade Organization.

Today, although those broad goals remain an important component of our national trade policy, the more immediate focus is on strengthening the Canada–U.S. partnership through closer, more formal, economic co-operation. A public debate on the issue has begun in Canada, one which I hope will also take hold in the United States. The central question in this debate is: What form should the Canada–U.S. partnership take?

At first glance, a stronger North American partnership may appear to be a cure for which there is no known disease. The concept lacks the political and philosophical appeal of European integration because the factors driving trilateral integration in North America are mostly economic, with the three countries explicitly avoiding political and cultural union. Nor is a closer relationship needed to protect against further hostilities between old enemies: There is no reason to fear military conflict between any of the countries.

> *The central question in this debate is: What form should the Canada–U.S. partnership take?*

Any relationship with the world's only remaining economic and military superpower is, by definition, a marriage of unequals. However, no attempt to create a continental community can succeed unless each country feels it is a full participant and is seen by its partners in that light.

Among Canadians, at least, there is little desire to emulate existing international models. Clearly, a made-in-North-America solution must be developed.

For the foreseeable future, the primary driver will continue to be economic. A new round of NAFTA negotiations could break down barriers that continue to distort investment and trade and drive up costs to consumers. There are many unfinished issues from the FTA and NAFTA, including anti-dumping, countervailing duties, agriculture, and, of course, softwood lumber. Integration cannot move forward without mechanisms both parties consider impartial and fair. The political and economic dominance of the United States, combined with interjurisdictional problems within Canada, makes developing such institutions particularly challenging. Given that it is sometimes easier to trade between Canada and the United States than between Canadian provinces, the scope of this problem is clear. In addition, it would be critical to design such institutions with a view to ultimately including the third NAFTA partner, Mexico.

A new North American partnership is inevitable. It will come either by default, as the forces of technology, commerce, and common security bind the three countries more closely together, or by design, if politicians, with advice and support from the business community among others, create a compelling vision of a true North American community.

South American Leaders to Set Goal of EU-like Union

By Tyler Bridges
The Seattle Times, December 12, 2004

A summit of South American leaders that began in Peru yesterday will pledge to merge the continent's two largest trading blocs over the next 10 to 15 years, with the eventual goal of creating a Latin American version of the European Union.

Plans to declare the birth of the South American Union have prompted cautions that it will amount to little more than the latest step toward unity in an endless road paved with good intentions.

"I don't want to be too downbeat, but I would be seriously surprised if they made any real progress," said Gary Hufbauer, a senior fellow at the Washington, D.C.–based Institute for International Economics. "That song has always had resonance, but it has never been strong enough to overcome genuine and deep protectionist policies."

Carlos Berninzon, a senior Peruvian diplomat, said the South American Union would be a continentwide free trade zone that would eliminate tariffs for "nonsensitive products" in 10 years and "sensitive products" in 15 years.

"The Andean community used to have its road," Berninzon said. "Mercosur used to have its road. Now the presidents of both organizations have agreed to establish a free trade zone between the two blocs."

The Andean Pact consists of Colombia, Ecuador, Peru, Venezuela, and Bolivia. Mercosur consists of Brazil, Argentina, Paraguay, and Uruguay.

The presidents or foreign ministers of the nine nations, plus observers from the governments of Mexico, Panama, Guyana, and Suriname are meeting in the Andean cities of Cuzco and Ayacucho.

Chile is not a full member of Mercosur—it's an associate member—because it adopted free trade policies in the 1970s and 1980s that its South American neighbors have been reluctant to accept, a sign of the difficulties of merging the various economies.

"There are all kinds of interesting ideas floating about, but there's not a lot of concrete action," said Riordan Roett, director of Western Hemisphere Affairs at Johns Hopkins University.

"Mercosur is hanging on by a thread. Its talks with the European Union have stalled. The Andean Pact doesn't function much anymore."

Eliminating tariffs and trade barriers inevitably hurts domestic companies that cannot compete against the foreign goods that would gain access to that country's market.

The interests that would suffer economically have had enough political sway in countries other than Chile to prevent fully liberalizing their economies.

"State intervention is declining," Hufbauer said, "but it's not close to withering away."

But even if the South American countries fail to formally create a union as envisioned, they are moving toward greater integration, led by Brazil, the continent's economic powerhouse.

Brazil has been extending loans to its neighbors to pave dirt roads and modernize ports.

Groups Defend California's Right to Protect Public Health

U.S. NEWSWIRE, MARCH 10, 2004

A coalition of environmental groups presented arguments today to the NAFTA dispute resolution panel hearing a foreign corporation's challenge to a California environmental regulation. In 1999, California decided to phase out MTBE, a gasoline additive suspected by the World Health Organization of being carcinogenic. MTBE has made its way into the groundwater supplies of hundreds of communities across the state, making the water undrinkable. The MTBE ban went into effect January 1, 2004.

Methanex Corporation, the Canadian parent company of a U.S. manufacturer of methanol, one component of MTBE, has brought a $970 million suit under NAFTA against the United States, demanding compensation for profits and business opportunities it claims to have lost because of California's phase-out. Such "investment protection" lawsuits are allowed under NAFTA's Chapter 11 rules.

Today's submission by Earthjustice on behalf of Bluewater Network, Communities for a Better Environment, and the Center for International Environmental Law, is the first time public concerns have been expressed directly in a NAFTA investment proceeding. The groups argued that international law requires the tribunal to respect the right of governments to take action to protect important public values like the right to clean water. The amicus submission was delivered to the International Centre for Settlement of Investment Disputes, administered by the World Bank in Washington, D.C.

"The state of California has both a right and an obligation to protect public health," said Martin Wagner, an attorney for Earthjustice who represented the groups. "Methanex's claim is tantamount to extortion, undermining health protections by demanding that the government pay nearly a billion dollars to protect citizens from harm. Our submission defends the right of California and all governments to protect public health and the environment without paying a fee to a corporation."

The threat presented by the Methanex case is further aggravated by the ongoing negotiations leading to the Free Trade of the Americas, an expansion of NAFTA's rules throughout the hemisphere. The agreement contains many of the same investor provisions that undermine regional decision-making and democracy.

"This would set the stage for a complete reversal of U.S. environmental law," said Adrienne Bloch of Communities for a Better Environment. "The United States is being sued for protecting people and the environment from a chemical that is destroying our drinking water supply. This one's a no-brainer."

"The Methanex arbitral tribunal has set an important precedent by recognizing its powers to accept submissions from civil society," said Marcos Orellana, an attorney with the Center for International Environmental Law (CIEL). "The millions of dollars likely spent by the United States in defending itself from Methanex's unwarranted claims further amplify the threats posed by the NAFTA Chapter 11 model to legitimate environmental and health measures, especially in the developing world."

"Even the process for challenges under NAFTA's Chapter 11 is undemocratic. It allows foreign corporations to challenge public health laws in tribunals designed to prioritize trade over the public health," said Elisa Lynch of Bluewater.

Background

NAFTA Tribunal: *Methanex v. United States of America*

Citizens Demand a Voice in Defense of Public Health

In October 2000, Earthjustice represented Bluewater Network and Communities for a Better Environment—environmental organizations that had worked to establish the California MTBE phase-out—as well as the Center for International Environmental Law in a petition to present their views to the tribunal hearing Methanex's NAFTA claim. Although international arbitration tribunals had never before permitted citizens to participate in these confidential processes—a point Methanex's lawyers highlighted to the tribunal—the groups convinced the tribunal that it had the authority to allow them to make written submissions in the case. The coalition filed that submission today.

Chapter 11: NAFTA's Little Secret

Methanex has argued that the California phase-out of MTBE violates special protections NAFTA's Chapter 11 provides to foreign investors. The Canadian firm Methanex, which operates a facility in the U.S., asserts that California's action was intended to favor Midwestern producers of ethanol—a potential substitute for MTBE—at the expense of foreign methanol manufacturers. If successful, Methanex could receive an award of nearly 1 billion dollars, paid by U.S. taxpayers.

MTBE: A Growing Public Health Issue

MTBE (methyl tertiary-butyl ether), a gasoline additive intended to lower air pollution, has been recognized as a threat to water quality and human health. Once MTBE enters the ground or surface water, it renders water unfit for human consumption. Even low concentrations can cause water to smell and taste like turpentine. The EPA acknowledges MTBE is a potential carcinogen. A University of California report estimated that at least 10,000 sites in California have been impacted by MTBE contamination. By 1996, the city of Santa Monica had to shut down half of its municipal wells—which served the city's 93,000 residents—because they had been contaminated with MTBE.

Trade Agreements Undermine Local Control

With the establishment of international investment rules like NAFTA's, national and state environmental laws are threatened by undemocratic procedures. NAFTA gives foreign investors unprecedented power to challenge national and state laws and to demand compensation when environmental or health measures affect the value of their investments. One of the most problematic aspects of

---

NAFTA gives foreign investors unprecedented power to challenge national and state laws and to demand compensation.

---

these provisions has been that they are exercised largely in secret. Investors' challenges to national regulations are decided in confidential arbitration proceedings, meaning the public can have no role in deciding the fate of democratically enacted health and environmental measures. The efforts of this coalition of environmentalists are helping to open these processes to the light of public scrutiny.

Because of the threat posed by MTBE, the California Senate and Assembly passed the MTBE Public Health and Environmental Protection Act in September 1997. The law called for the University of California to evaluate the human health and environmental risks of the use of MTBE in gasoline, and for the governor to take appropriate action in response to the findings. The study concluded that the use of MTBE in gasoline posed a "significant risk" to California's environment. As a result, in 1999 the governor ordered MTBE to be removed from gasoline by the end of 2002.

This is where the international investment rules come into play. Three months after the governor announced the MTBE ban, a Canadian corporation called Methanex, which manufactures one component of MTBE (methanol), filed a claim against the United States demanding $970 million if California insisted on following through with its MTBE ban.

Methanex's Claims

First, Methanex argued that California's action had taken away future profits it was entitled to, violating NAFTA's prohibition against what is called "expropriation." The concept of expropriation is international law's version of what U.S. law calls protection against "takings." The principle is straightforward: the government can take private property for the benefit of society at large—as when it decides it needs to build a highway in a certain area of private property—but it must pay fair compensation. However, under international law no compensation is due where a government regulates in the public interest for the protection of health and the environment.

U.S. courts have recognized limitations to that rule, however, because governments could not carry out their responsibility to promote the common good if they had to pay every time government action impacts private property. As the Supreme Court has said, the impacts of regulations protecting important public interests "are the burdens we must all bear in exchange for the advantage of living and doing business in a civilized community." Methanex argued that NAFTA does not contain the same limitation as U.S. law, and that it was therefore entitled to compensation it could not obtain in U.S. courts.

Methanex's second concern was its belief that California's ban was intended not to protect health or the environment, but to remove foreign competition for U.S. (mostly Midwestern) producers of ethanol, one likely candidate to replace MTBE in gasoline. NAFTA requires that foreign investors receive treatment "no less favorable" than domestic ones. Methanex was not deterred by California's claim that it did not intend to add ethanol to its gasoline (in fact, the state sought permission from the federal government not to replace MTBE with any additive).

In August 2002, the NAFTA tribunal dismissed most of Methanex's claims on the ground that its investment in methanol production was not tied closely enough to California's ban on MTBE. The tribunal was concerned, however, about Methanex's allegations of discrimination and allowed the case to go forward on that basis.

Trade Tribunals Undermine Democracy and Open Government

The Methanex NAFTA case raises important public policy issues. Instead of resolving those issues in processes open to full public participation, as do most U.S. courts, international investment tribunals decide them in relative secret with little if any opportunity for a full airing of the issues. The tribunal's decision in the Methanex case will have precedential effect that will help determine the rights and obligations of governments in implementing future health and environmental measures.

A decision requiring the United States to compensate Methanex would not only pressure California to rescind important environmental and health measures, but would also compromise the legitimate powers of governments to protect the health, safety, and environment of their citizens. Commercial trade agreements would be empowered to trump local, regional, state, and, eventually, federal health and environmental standards.

Bibliography

Books

Appleton, Barry. *Navigating NAFTA: A Concise User's Guide to the North American Free Trade Agreement.* Rochester, N.Y.: Lawyers Cooperative Pub., 1994.

Barry, Tom. *Zapata's Revenge: Free Trade and the Farm Crisis in Mexico.* Boston: South End Press, 1995.

Bhagwati, Jagdish. *In Defense of Globalization.* New York: Oxford University Press, 2004.

Brown, Sherrod. *Myths of Free Trade: Why American Trade Policy Has Failed.* New York: New Press, 2004.

Bulmer-Thomas, Victor, Nikki Craske, and Mónica Serrano, eds. *Mexico and the North American Free Trade Agreement: Who Will Benefit?* New York: St. Martin's Press, 1994.

Conti, Delia B. *Reconciling Free Trade, Fair Trade, and Interdependence: The Rhetoric of Presidential Economic Leadership.* Westport, Conn.: Praeger, 1998.

Davis, Christina L. *Food Fights over Free Trade: How International Institutions Promote Agricultural Trade Liberalization.* Princeton: Princeton University Press, 2003.

Folsom, Ralph H. *NAFTA and Free Trade in the Americas in a Nutshell.* 2nd ed. St. Paul, Minn.: Thomson/West, 2004.

Galal, Ahmed, and Robert Z. Lawrence, eds. *Building Bridges: An Egypt–U.S. Free Trade Agreement.* Washington, D.C.: Brookings Institution, 1998.

Gallagher, Kevin P. *Free Trade and the Environment: Mexico, NAFTA, and Beyond.* Stanford: Stanford Law and Politics, 2004.

Gereffi, Gary, David Spener, and Jennifer Bair, eds. *Free Trade and Uneven Development: The North American Apparel Industry After NAFTA.* Philadelphia: Temple University Press, 2002.

Grinspun, Ricardo, and Maxwell A. Cameron, eds. *The Political Economy of North American Free Trade.* New York: St. Martin's Press, 1993.

Holbein, James R., and Nick W. Ranieri, eds. *The EU-Mexico Free Trade Agreement.* Ardsley, N.Y.: Transnational Publishers, 2002.

Irwin, Douglas A. *Free Trade Under Fire.* 2nd ed. Princeton, N.J.: Princeton University Press, 2005.

Koh, Tommy, and Chang Li Lin, eds. *The United States Singapore Free Trade Agreement: Highlights and Insights.* Singapore: World Scientific, 2004.

Kreinin, Mordechai E., ed. *Building a Partnership: The Canada–United States Free Trade Agreement.* East Lansing: Michigan State University Press, 2000.

Lusztig, Michael. *The Limits of Protectionism: Building Coalitions for Free Trade.* Pittsburgh: University of Pittsburgh Press, 2004.

MacArthur, John R. *The Selling of "Free Trade": NAFTA, Washington, and the Subversion of American Democracy*. New York: Hill and Wang, 2000.

MacDonald, L. Ian, ed. *Free Trade: Risks and Rewards*. Montreal: McGill–Queen's University Press, 2000.

Marceau, Gabrielle. *Anti-dumping and Anti-trust Issues in Free-Trade Areas*. New York: Oxford University Press, 1994.

Miller, Henrí, ed. *Free Trade Versus Protectionism*. New York: H.W. Wilson Co., 1996.

Nader, Ralph, et al. *The Case Against "Free Trade": GATT, NAFTA, and the Globalization of Corporate Power*. Berkeley, Calif.: North Atlantic Books, 1993.

Nesadurai, Helen E.S., *Globalisation, Domestic Politics, and Regionalism: The ASEAN Free Trade Area*. New York: Routledge, 2003.

Ross, Andrew, ed. *No Sweat: Fashion, Free Trade, and the Rights of Garment Workers*. New York: Verso, 1997.

Salazar-Xirinachs, José Manuel, and Maryse Robert, eds. *Toward Free Trade in the Americas*. Washington, D.C.: Brookings Institution Press, Organization of American States, 2001.

Schott, Jeffrey J., ed. *Free Trade Agreements: U.S. Strategies and Priorities*. Washington, D.C.: Institute for International Economics, 2004.

Thacker, Strom C. *Big Business, the State, and Free Trade: Constructing Coalitions in Mexico*. New York: Cambridge University Press, 2000.

Tonelson, Alan. *The Race to the Bottom: Why a Worldwide Worker Surplus and Uncontrolled Free Trade Are Sinking American Living Standards*. Boulder, Colo.: Westview Press, 2000.

Urmetzer, Peter. *From Free Trade to Forced Trade: Canada in the Global Economy*. New York: Penguin Canada, 2003.

Weintraub, Sidney, Alan M. Rugman, and Gavin Boyd. *Free Trade in the Americas: Economic and Political Issues for Governments and Firms*. Northampton, Mass.: Edward Elgar, 2004.

Zeiler, Thomas W. *Free Trade, Free World: The Advent of GATT*. Chapel Hill: University of North Carolina Press, 1999.

Web Sites

This section offers the reader a list of Web sites that can provide more extensive information on free trade, NAFTA, and arguments for and against free trade agreements (FTAs). These Web sites also include links to other sites that may be of help or interest. Due to the nature of the Internet, the continued existence of a site is never guaranteed, but at the time of this book's publication, all of these Internet addresses were in operation.

NAFTA Secretariat
www.nafta-sec-alena.org

Official Web site of the North American Free Trade Agreement. It contains information on the dispute settlement proceedings, legal texts, and panel decisions and reports concerning NAFTA.

United States–Mexico Chamber of Commerce
www.usmcoc.org/n1.html

Provides information on Mexico and U.S.–Mexico relations. The site mainly concerns NAFTA and other FTAs.

World Trade Organization (WTO)
www.wto.org

The official Web site of the WTO, the international body that deals with the rules of trade between nations.

Proponents of Free Trade

The Center for Trade Policy Studies
www.freetrade.org

The Cato Institute's free trade Web site. The mission of the Center for Trade Policy Studies is to increase public understanding of the benefits of free trade and the costs of protectionism.

Foundation for Economic Education
www.fee.org

The foundation's mission is to educate the world on the principles of free-market economics.

The Future of Freedom Foundation
www.fff.org

Attempts to provides the moral, philosophical, and economic case for liberty, free markets, private property, and limited government.

Global Growth Org (London)

www.global-growth.org/

Campaigns against the causes of poverty in developing countries. The organization advocates lasting solutions to the structural economic, political, and cultural causes of poverty. It believes that trade can unite mankind in peace and prosperity.

The Heritage Foundation

www.heritage.org/Research/TradeandForeignAid/index.cfm

This Web page of the Heritage Foundation's official site explores how expanding global trade can help build a stronger economy in the United States and promote better relationships abroad by fighting poverty and hunger in the world's poorer nations.

Tech Central Station

www.techcentralstation.com

Tech Central Station looks at the public policy implications of technology and the way technology is changing and shaping the world.

Opponents of Free Trade

Free Trade and Globalization

www.globalissues.org/TradeRelated/FreeTrade.asp

Provides arguments that are critical of free trade and the WTO, and provides links to further information.

Gone with the World

www.gonewiththeworld.com

Seeks to inform people of the dangers and disruptions of globalization, free trade, and the outsourcing of jobs.

Oxfam

www.oxfam.org.uk/coolplanet/milkingit/information/the_issues/free_trade.htm

This site—the official site of Oxfam, which works with other groups to overcome poverty and suffering around the world—looks critically at the philosophy behind free trade and asks whether trade can be made freer and more fair for poor countries.

U.S. Reform Party

www.reformparty.org/cgi-bin/hcgmain.cgi

This party believes that the United States should negotiate trade agreements that promote American jobs, consumer safety, environmental protection, and fair trade.

Additional Periodical Articles with Abstracts

More information about free trade and related subjects can be found in the following articles. Readers who require a more comprehensive selection are advised to consult *Business Abstracts*, *Humanities Abstracts*, *Readers' Guide Abstracts*, *Social Science Abstracts*, and other H.W. Wilson publications.

Fading Faith in Free Trade. Robert E. Senser. *America*, v. 191 pp13–16 July 5–12, 2004.

According to Senser, America's elites, and even the general public, are beginning to raise serious questions about the country's free trade consensus. A poll conducted nationwide in January 2004 by the University of Maryland's Program on International Policy Alternatives reveals that most people in the United States support expanding trade but favor changes in the U.S. government's trade-related policies. Moreover, even the consensus favoring free trade among the elites has lately been questioned, writes Senser, and some of the policies of the international network of trade institutions built under that consensus are being challenged. Senser expected U.S. foreign trade and employment policies, a central campaign issue in the 2004 presidential election, to prompt a spirited and frank discussion by the candidates.

An Imbalance of Power. Cesar Ferrari and Carlos Novoa. *America*, v. 190 pp20–23 March 1, 2004.

The writers argue that American agricultural subsidies are a threat to free trade. In September 2003 the ministerial meeting of the World Trade Organization in Cancun, Mexico, collapsed because the agreed-upon agenda was overpowered by issues favorable to America, Europe, and Japan. The issues of state procurements, foreign investment, intellectual property, and competition were given greater significance than the issue of agricultural subsidies—the range of financial support programs that developed nations use to strengthen their agricultural economies. According to the writers, these subsidies hinder the sale of the agricultural products of developing countries, which are frequently their main export, within the markets of the developed world.

Chile—A Giant Step Toward Free Trade Across the Americas? Geri Smith. *Business Week*, p53 June 16, 2003.

Smith writes that the U.S.–Chile free trade agreement is an important step forward for U.S. policy in Latin America. The pact, expected to be approved by Congress in fall 2003, is designed to eliminate tariffs on 85 percent of goods traded between the two countries and provide protections for such U.S. intellectual property exports as software and pharmaceuticals. U.S. trade representative Robert B. Zoellick hopes that the agreement will prompt hitherto-reluctant Latin countries to move faster to approve a hemisphere-wide deal that would cut tariffs, guarantee investors' rights, and boost U.S. business in the region.

The Pernicious Rise of "Core Europe." John Rossant. *Business Week*, p57 May 10, 2004.

Some German and French policymakers are talking about Core Europe, a narrow region revolving around France and Germany, with Spain, the Benelux countries, and perhaps eventually Italy playing supporting roles, says Rossant. Core Europe is distinct from the pro-American British, with their free trade notions, and the poor new members arriving from central Europe. According to Rossant, Core Europe's precepts are a sort of protectionism lite—which promotes national champions and uses market methods to advance its dirigiste goals when necessary—and a determination to keep U.S. influence in check while bending EU rules to promote the interests of the core.

Trade Not Aid. *Canada and the World Backgrounder*, v. 69 pp12–15 September 2003.

The article claims that many developing nations find that they are unable to trade with the world's economic giants unless they sell their natural resources at a low price. Research by the World Bank indicates that opening markets would do more to assist poor nations than development assistance can ever hope to achieve. OXFAM notes that the markets in sugar, coffee, cotton, and other commodities that tropical farmers can grow at low cost are distorted by subsidies of $300 billion per year to growers in the rich world. Critics of the current system are not opposed to free trade, but they are in favor of trade policies that benefit everyone.

The U.S. & Free Trade. Jay Mandle. *Commonweal*, v. 130 pp8–9 October 24, 2003.

Mandle argues that the United States' retreat from multilateralism at the World Trade Organization negotiations in Cancun, Mexico, in September is shortsighted. The spread of economic growth has meant that, for the first time, relatively poor nations have gained an important role in international trade negotiations. According to Mandle, their success in penetrating export markets has created a protectionist reaction in the United States, which has resisted the logic of free trade and economic efficiency, particularly in aiming to protect its steel, textile, and agricultural sectors. America's unilateralism, he says, sacrifices the prospect of raising the country's own income levels, even as farmers in poor countries are blocked from opportunities to raise theirs.

Free Trade Is a Big Issue for Consumers. Daniel T. Griswold. *Consumers' Research Magazine*, v. 86 pp16–17 October 2003.

Griswold writes that consumers derive huge benefits from the freedom to buy goods and services in a global marketplace. Like domestic competition, he says, the competition that international trade brings to the U.S. economy means lower prices, better quality, and more variety. A recent study from the Federal Reserve Bank of Dallas reported that prices fell between 1997 and 2002 for products subject to the most import competition, such as TVs, toys, roasted coffee, clothing and footwear, cars, and video, photographic, and audio equipment. Unfortunately, according to Griswold, whenever trade is discussed in Washington, the focus is almost entirely on its effect on producers and jobs, not on consumers.

NAFTA at 10: Plus or a Minus? Jorge G. Castaneda. *Current History*, v. 103 pp51–55 February 2004.

The North American Free Trade Agreement (NAFTA) has been neither the win-win situation that some of its proponents believed it would be nor the catastrophe that its critics predicted, writes Castaneda. When they drafted NAFTA a decade ago, the United States, Mexico, and Canada agreed to lift trade barriers and create a region in which trade, commerce, and investment would take center stage in their relationships. Among other things, NAFTA has linked Mexico's economy ever more closely to the United States, causing the former to become far more reliant on the American economy's health. Castaneda says that, as many have predicted, increased economic integration has expanded international trade, but it has not resulted in improved standards of living in Mexico.

How Green Is NAFTA? Measuring the Impacts of Agricultural Trade. Scott Vaughan. *Environment*, v. 46 pp26–42 March 2004.

A decade after the North American Free Trade Agreement (NAFTA) came into being, says Vaughan, both it and its parallel environmental accord remain subjects of intense debate. Trade affects environmental quality by increasing the scale of economic activity, and it influences environmental policy by affecting domestic food safety policies or environmental and conservation regulations that seek to condition the market access of goods based on their environmental characteristics. The debate over NAFTA is centered on this latter area, writes Vaughan, as environmentalists fear that trade will weaken hard-won environmental laws, while developing countries oppose any imposition of the same environmental standards as those imposed on industrialized nations as a precondition of market access. The effects of NAFTA-related liberalization of Mexico's agricultural sector on nitrogen pollution, water scarcity, and biological diversity loss are analyzed.

The Protectionist Threat. A. Gary Shilling. *Forbes*, v. 172 p268 November 24, 2003.

Shilling contends that the United States should be careful not to introduce creeping protectionism. The Bush administration's approach to keeping free trade alive is to push bilateral deals. Agreements have been made with Chile and Singapore—with an additional 14 under discussion—and the 10 members of the Association of Southeast Asian Nations (ASEAN) are dedicated to a free trade zone by 2020. The problem with bilateral and regional trade agreements, however, Shilling writes, is that they are exclusionary and little better than tariffs. Regardless of intentions, he claims, protectionism is ultimately bad for jobs, the economy, profits, and shares.

Mend the Crack and Put Doha Back on Track. Ernesto Zedillo. *Forbes*, v. 171 p35 June 23, 2003.

Of the many outstanding issues on the international agenda, Zedillo argues, none deserves more attention than the World Trade Organization Doha Round, launched in November 2001. This was supposed to be the round in which negotiators would seriously address the issues of greatest interest to developing nations, but those countries were skeptical of the sincerity of the rich countries in this regard. This deadlock must be broken, claims Zedillo, because the goals of the Doha Round are important in themselves and because failure to progress will add fuel to the already fierce fire of trade disputes and flagrant abuse of trade safeguards by both developed and developing nations.

Cancun's False Promise: A View from the South. Benjamin William Mkapa. *Foreign Affairs*, v. 83 pp133–35 May/June 2004.

In a letter to the editor, Benjamin William Mkapa, president of the United Republic of Tanzania, responds to the article "Don't Cry for Cancun," which appeared in the January/February issue. He states that the only positive aspect for the poor in the World Trade Organization talks in Cancun last September was the unprecedented show of unity among developing countries. He says that the world can achieve a global trading system that is open and fair, that rewards initiative and entrepreneurship, that helps finance development, and that can earn the support of people in the developing world, but in order to achieve this, governments must focus on making coherent and coordinated trade policy that is consistent with the Millennium Development Goals, which were unanimously adopted by the UN in 2000.

The Unlikely Trade Warrior. Justin Fox. *Fortune*, v. 148 pp41–42 December 8, 2003.

Although President Bush never aimed to be a protectionist, Fox writes, his presidency is becoming obstructive to free trade. The 2001 recession prompted Bush to impose a 30 percent tariff on steel imports in 2002 and to sign a farm bill packed with protectionist measures designed to promote free trade through forums, such as the World Trade Organization, while securing publicity and votes. The problem with this split policy, according to Fox, is that Bush is not the only world leader who is answerable to an electorate concerned about jobs and nervous about foreigners. Indeed, Fox claims, voters abroad happen to be, as a rule, particularly suspicious of Bush and constantly seek signs of U.S. hypocrisy, which means that few of the president's foreign counterparts have any political incentive to cut him slack on trade.

The Economics of Empire. William Finnegan. *Harper's*, v. 306 pp41–54 May 2003.

The Bush administration has a transcendent commitment to the idea of "free trade," says Finnegan. This dogma is promulgated directly through U.S. foreign policy and indirectly through multilateral institutions, such as the World Bank, the IMF, and the World Trade Organization. According to Finnegan, its fundamental tenets are deregulation, privatization, "openness" to foreign investment and imports, unrestricted movement of capital, and lower taxes. Presented with special force to developing countries as a recipe for economic management, it is also, in its entirety, a theory of how the world should be run, under American supervision. The writer discusses how countries such as Bolivia have suffered because of America's promotion of "free trade."

Free Trade Blues. Mary Janigan. *Maclean's*, v. 116 p12 December 22, 2003.

Fed up with the lack of progress toward freer world trade, countries are increasingly forging regional and bilateral trade pacts, partitioning the globe with almost 300 sophisticated treaties, Janigan reports. In 2003 alone, 12 deals have been signed, nine are in talks, and 13 others have been suggested. These figures, says Janigan, reinforce the worst fears of global trade supporters: The drive toward an expanded WTO deal covering everything from agricultural subsidies to investment is on the back burner, perhaps for years.

A Spectacular Success? Eric Alterman. *The Nation*, v. 278 p10 February 2, 2004.

Alterman reports that, on the 10th anniversary of the NAFTA accord, mainstream media accounts have expressed muted disappointment with its comparatively slight effects. A Carnegie Endowment study revealed that the accord did not come close to creating the amount of jobs it was expected to generate in Mexico. Instead, it devastated hundreds of thousands of Mexico's subsistence farmers and had little effect on jobs in the United States. At the same time, writes Alterman, the expected advantages of the accord—that it would improve intra-American relations and reduce Mexican resentment toward their immense northern neighbor—have been more than offset by the costs of America's other actions.

From Seattle to Miami. Sarah Anderson and John Cavanagh. *The Nation*, v. 277 pp5–6 December 1, 2003.

The writers argue that the talks on the Free Trade Area of the Americas (FTAA) will probably be very different from those held nine years ago. At the last gathering, President Clinton assembled 33 of his Western Hemisphere counterparts for a variety of elaborate forms of entertainment and a harmonious discussion of plans for the trade deal. Since then, the writers say, the pendulum of power between free trade supporters and their opponents has swung wildly, and the so-called Washington consensus model of corporate globalization has been battered by stunning corporate scandals, the failed promises of NAFTA, and the financial scandals of the late 1990s. The consequent crisis of legitimacy, report the writers, has afforded protesters and governments of poor nations the possibility of stalemating the World Trade Organization and defeating the proposed FTAA.

Global Fights Go Local. John Nichols. *The Nation* v. 279 p22 August 30–September 6, 2004.

According to Nichols, the debate over trade and economic globalization issues is moving to the states, as are debates on numerous issues previously regarded as the exclusive province of federal officials. Although Congress is still the main battleground in conflicts over free trade agreements and tax policies that are advantageous to the "Benedict Arnold" corporations that John Kerry criticized for transferring jobs to countries with low wages and less stringent environmental regulations, state officials are often the first to face pressure when factories shut down and service jobs are outsourced, Nichols says.

Trading Up: Cambodia's Improved Labor Conditions. Sheridan Prasso. *The New Republic*, v. 231 pp11–12 August 16–23, 2004.

Prasso reports that an unprecedented trade experiment is being tested in Cambodia, but it is the last of such trade deals because the Bush administration opposes such connections. Garment workers in Phnom Penh are well-paid by local standards and enjoy working conditions certified by the International Labor Organization (ILO) as being in "substantial compliance" with the highest labor standards. In 1999 the United States and Cambodia signed an agreement connecting U.S. garment quotas to ILO-certified improvements in factory working conditions in Cambodia; the more the country improved its labor conditions, the more access it would have to U.S. markets. It is a shame, argues Prasso, that this type of agreement has not been repeated, because Cambodia's test case has generally been a success both economically and morally.

Winners and Losers. John Cassidy. *The New Yorker*, v. 80 pp26–30 August 2, 2004.

Ensuring the United States' prosperity in the global marketplace involves investing in the nation's human, social, and cultural capital, Cassidy writes. Today, largely due to digitization and the Internet, the service sector, which employs four-fifths of the labor force, is increasingly affected by global labor arbitrage. Many white-collar industries that once offered safe and well-paid jobs, such as telecommunications, insurance, and stockbroking, are no longer safe from the temptation to outsource. If the United States is to meet the challenge posed by a genuine world economy, Cassidy argues, it will have to make sure that its scientists are the most creative, its business leaders the most innovative, and its workers the most highly skilled, a difficult task when other countries are seeking the same goals. According to Cassidy, a truly enlightened trade policy would involve, among other things, increasing federal support for science at all levels of the education system, creating financial incentives for companies to pursue technological innovation, and encouraging the development of the arts.

10 Truths About Trade: Global Trade and American Jobs. Brink Lindsey. *Reason*, v. 36 pp24–31 July 2004.

Lindsey contends that the recent scare about "offshoring" is only the latest twist on a dubious, decades-old complaint that global trade is stealing jobs and resulting in corporations relentlessly searching the world for the lowest wages and most squalid working conditions. In truth, says Lindsey, trade is just one element in a much bigger picture of continuous turnover in the U.S. labor market, and the overall trend is toward more and better jobs for U.S. workers. Some basic truths about global trade and U.S. jobs, the writer says, are that the number of jobs grows with the population, jobs change constantly, high-paying and challenging jobs are becoming more plentiful, "deindustrialization" is a myth, and imports have not been a major cause of recent manufacturing job losses.

U.S. Court Opens Door to Free Trade in Ideas. David Malakoff. *Science*, v. 301 p1643 September 19, 2003.

A recent U.S. court decision makes it easier for U.S. scientists to import scientific knowledge, reports Malakoff. The court case involved a dispute between Housey Pharmaceuticals of Southfield, Michigan, and European drug giant Bayer AG over Bayer's use of a protein screening process on which Housey holds a U.S. patent. Housey demanded royalties from Bayer under a 1988 U.S. law that bars companies from freely importing products made by a process patented in the U.S. An appeals court dismissed Housey's claim by explaining that the 1988 law is limited to physical goods that were manufactured and does not include information.

Tug-of-War over Trade. Matt Forney. *Time*, v. 162 pp42–44 December 22, 2003.

According to Forney, U.S. manufacturers are suffering as China becomes the world's factory. A massive pool of cheap labor is expected to fuel growth for another 20 years in the Chinese economy, which already produces a quarter of the world's television sets and washing machines and half of its cameras and photocopiers. A number of U.S. towns have been devastated as companies move their whole operations to China, and some U.S. manufacturers are calling for protectionist policies against Chinese imports. Forney explains that Washington has to walk a tightrope, however, because China is the fastest-growing market for America's exports, and the country needs China's cooperation on everything from trying to shut down North Korea's weapons program to building support for Iraq policy in the UN.

A Failing Grade on Global Trade. Kevin Clarke. *U.S. Catholic*, v. 69 p36 March 2004.

The North American Free Trade Agreement (NAFTA) is not working to end poverty in the way that its supporters said that it would, writes Clarke. America, Canada, and Mexico have enjoyed more trade and some minor economic growth because of NAFTA, which was signed during the Clinton administration. None of that new wealth has gone to the manufacturing zones that are dying across the United States, however, argues Clarke, or to the abandoned cornfields of native farmers in southern Mexico. Although international trade may generate wealth, it does not control how it is distributed, and the rewards of worldwide commerce and the economic growth that it creates are too often reserved for those who are already wealthy.

The Imbalance of Trade. Lou Dobbs. *U.S. News & World Report*, v. 136 p46 April 5, 2004.

Dobbs writes that President Bush and many of his cabinet members are attempting to change the national debate on the cost of free trade, outsourcing of U.S. jobs to cheap overseas labor markets, and responsible trade policies. Advocates of free trade have for the past 30 years envisioned a border-free society, with trade being the great equalizer as well as the driver for unbounded global prosperity, but U.S. trade policies have failed to live up to utopian promises, says Dobbs. The U.S. multinationals now want to be able to outsource jobs to inexpensive overseas labor markets with little apparent regard for Americans who lose their jobs. Furthermore, the government argues it does not need to follow rational trade policies because any change in policy would interfere with free trade. According to Dobbs, the initial response of the White House to the growing national debate on trade policy and international business labor practices has been to label as economic isolationists those who are looking for a balanced trade policy, as if there were no middle ground in pursuing U.S. interests.

"We Are All Zapatistas." Leif Utne. *Utne,* pp36–37 November/December 2003.

Utne writes that the Mexican insurgents known as "Zapatistas" are reinventing global politics. On January 1, 1994, barely half an hour after the North American Free Trade Agreement (NAFTA) had gone into effect, 3,000 masked rebels took control of seven towns in the jungles of Mexico's southern state of Chiapas. Named after Emiliano Zapata, hero of the Mexican Revolution of 1910, these insurgents were pursued by 15,000 Mexican soldiers, but a surge of public sympathy compelled President Carlos Salinas de Gortari to call off his troops. The Zapatistas were not the first group to target the power of multinational corporations, says Utne, but by focusing their efforts on NAFTA and encouraging "civil society" to get involved in the struggle, they were the first organized popular uprising against the entire neoliberal economic order.

Free Trade at Last? Gregory Mastel. *Weekly Standard,* v. 8 pp18–19 June 2, 2003.

Recent trends and events suggest that it is time for the United States to introduce a free trade agreement (FTA) with Taiwan, argues Mastel. The United States and Taiwan have disputed the size of the bilateral trade imbalance, agriculture, and intellectual property protections. Nonetheless, Mastel writes, their large and expanding economic relationship has been advantageous to the United States and instrumental in Taiwan's transition to democracy. According to Mastel, America should keep pursuing a realistic and responsible framework for policy toward Taiwan that advances the countries' mutual interests, then build an economic bridge between Washington and Taipei in the form of a new free trade agreement. This will allow both countries to build their economies, he says, encourage further reform in Taiwan, and cement a core relationship between free market democracies.

A Taste of Our Own Poison. Lawrence Lessig. *Wired,* v. 12 p109 January 2004.

America's drive to protect intellectual property is defended as simply one aspect of free trade—the aspect that benefits Hollywood—but America does not respect the free trade rules that it imposes on others, Lessig contends. Whereas the United States invokes free trade to defend intellectual property safeguards, it obstructs the free trade that developing countries are most concerned with—agriculture—by subsidizing U.S. farming for $300 billion per year. Developing nations cannot do much about this situation individually, but more and more they are acting together. One group recently left trade talks because agribusiness subsidies were not under discussion, and others are openly considering ways to get America's attention. The writer discusses one way for the developing nations to empower themselves.

NAFTA and Mexico's 10-Year Lethargy. Pablo Marentes. *World Press Review*, v. 51 p47 March 2004.

In an article excerpted from the January 6, 2004, issue of *El Universal* of Mexico City, the writer argues that after 10 years, the Mexican economy has yet to benefit from the North American Free Trade Agreement and that the country is still overshadowed by the hegemony of the United States.

South America: Free Trade at the Crossroads. Robert Taylor. *World Press Review*, v. 51 p27 January 2004.

The writer examines the coverage given by five South American newspapers to the possible collapse of the Free Trade Area of the Americas initiative. On the eve of a meeting of FTAA negotiating teams in Miami, Florida, in November 2003, correspondent Andres Oppenheimer cautioned in *La Nacion* of Buenos Aires that President Bush's top Latin American advisers are pushing a "tough love" policy. Debate has been especially heated in Brazil, which irritated Washington when the government of Luiz Inacio Lula da Silva strenuously criticized U.S. agricultural subsidies as a hindrance to trade liberalization.

Index